THE

GREAT

SENDING

THE
GREAT
SENDING

GOD'S HEART FOR THE WORLD
BEATING THROUGH
YOU

WILL SOHNS

TENTH
POWER

ELGIN, IL

TENTHPOWERPUBLISHING

www.tenthpowerpublishing.com

All proceeds of this publication, a non-profit endeavor, will go toward reimbursing the marketing and publication costs incurred by Resurrection Lutheran Church, Spring, Texas. Any proceeds that exceed the costs of reimbursement will support Harvest Partnership (a church planting network in greater Houston) and/or any other such church planting mission that participates in Christ's great sending into the world. Authors receive no remuneration.

Design by Inkwell Creative

Softcover ISBN 978-1-938840-42-5

e-book ISBN 978-1-938840-43-2

10 9 8 7 6 5 4 3 2 1

To Jesus Christ Who was sent with the authority to give eternal life to the world (John 17:1-5).

To all in the world who will become Christ-believers through the power of the Gospel (Romans 1:16) and will be united with Christ and His love (John 17:20-26).

To all fellow believer-disciples who have been sanctified in the Gospel truth to be sent ones of Christ into the world. God's heart is beating through them (John 17:6-19).

To all Evangelical Lutherans who have benefited from the Scriptural Reformation (1517) to this day (Romans 3:21-28; Ephesians 2:8-10) and who are sent into the world together with other Christians in the world.

To all the biological and Christ-families of *The Great Sending* contributors (John 17; Ephesians 2:11-22).

To all current and former District Presidents of the Lutheran Church—Missouri Synod who wholeheartedly supported *The Great Sending.*

As the Father has sent me, I am sending you. —John 20:21

TABLE OF CONTENTS

CHAPTER 2

ENGAGING DISCIPLES IN THE GREAT SENDING

CHAPTER 3

THE GREAT CHRIST SENDING

CHAPTER 4

THE GREAT SENDING ESSENTIALS

ACKNOWLEDGMENTS

The God Who loves us all in Christ Jesus is to be acknowledged above all. He alone is due the credit for this work. For we are his workmanship, created in Christ Jesus for good works, which God prepared beforehand, that we should walk in them (Ephesians 2:10).

This *Missio Dei* initiative acknowledges that it is the very *Missio Dei* – the Sending of God – and His Word that creates and shapes God's people to be co-heirs and co-associates with Him in His sending.

With that acknowledgment, the following people have formed the missional background and focus for this initiative: the missionally immersed biological families of the author and contributors, their church families, and their colleagues throughout the years.

Included among God's instruments for the missional nature and shaping are many congregations of all sizes – small to large – and their pastors. In addition, we give God the glory for the missional salutary influence of mega churches and their pastors; the Pastoral Leadership Institute (PLI); Lutheran Bible Translators (LBT); Best Practices for Ministry and others.

Deserving special acknowledgement are all who assisted with, contributed to and/or supported this project, especially the consortium of 15 contributors, who did not receive any remuneration for their work; Rev. Dr. Steve Sohns and Resurrection Lutheran Church, Spring, Texas, for offering insight and the financial resources to make this publication possible; publisher Jim Galvin; and editor Kate Meadows.

Encouragement and engagement came from 34 former District President colleagues, among whom are one former President and four former Vice Presidents of the Lutheran Church—Missouri Synod. Many other former and current colleagues have provided leadership and supported this ground-breaking *Missio Dei* immersion, including numerous current District Presidents.

SOLI DEO GLORIA

In Christ and His love,

Will Sohns
General Editor

CONTRIBUTORS

A Consortium of Missional Authors

The contributors to *The Great Sending* are recognized missional leaders of the Lutheran Church—Missouri Synod, fourteen of whom are former officials and one of whom is a current official. All fifteen are recognized as having God's heart for the world beating through them.

- Rev. Dr. David H. Benke, former District President
- Rev. Dr. David Buegler, former District President and former Synod Vice-President
- Rev. Dr. Jon Diefenthaler, former District President
- Rev. Ken Hennings, former District President and former chairman, the Council of Presidents
- Rev. Dr. Gerald B. (Jerry) Kieschnick, former District President, former Synod President and former chairman, the International Lutheran Council
- The Rev. Keith Kohlmeier, former District President
- Rev. Dr. David P. E. Maier, current District President and current chairman, the Council of Presidents
- Rev. Dr. Paul L. Maier, former Synod Vice-President
- Rev. Dr. Dale A. Meyer, former Synod Vice-President and former President of Concordia Seminary, St. Louis
- Rev. Dr. Gerhard C. Michael, Jr., former District President

- Rev. Dr. Dean Nadasdy, former District President and former Synod Vice-President
- Rev. Dr. Robert Newton, former District President
- Rev. Dr. Wilbert J. Sohns, former District President
- Rev. Dr. Russ Sommerfeld, former District President
- Rev. Dr. Larry Stoterau, former District President and former chairman, the Council of Presidents

See contributor biographies under Missiological Resources for The Great Sending.

PREFACE

A Jubilee – Immersed in the Missio Dei

During my fifty years as a pastor in The Lutheran Church—Missouri Synod, I've often wondered what it would take to reverse the trend that had already begun before my ordination in 1970. That trend was a slow but steady decline in the number of members in LCMS congregations.

The four congregations I served comprised faithful people who loved the Lord Jesus and who, for the most part, were faithful in worship, Bible study, and reception of the Lord's Supper. Each of those congregations grew incrementally but not exponentially.

My role as ecclesiastical supervisor and church leader provided opportunity to hear from many pastors and lay leaders the blessings and difficulties their congregations were experiencing. Some were growing slowly. Others were declining steadily. Very few were expanding rapidly.

My question during those years was a simple one: Why? Why were most of our churches not enjoying the kind of rapid growth described in the book of Acts? What was happening in the church two thousand years ago that's not happening today? And what can be done to reverse that trend?

My conclusion is also a simple one: Many in the church today have lost the sense of purpose so clearly understood by the first Christians. The first Christians knew Jesus personally. They lived with him and learned from him. They saw him die. They witnessed his resurrection. He said he would come back. They believed him and led their lives as if he were going to return during their lifetime.

That was two thousand years ago and he still hasn't come back. Yet his message is just as relevant, just as urgent as it was back then: "You will be my witnesses... to the ends of the earth" (Acts 1:8); and, "As my father has sent me, even so I am sending you" (John 20:21).

Respectfully I commend to you this special resource, prepared by faithful, missional, passionate pastors and church leaders. We, like you, are sent by God: "We are therefore Christ's ambassadors, as though God were making his appeal through us. We implore you on Christ's behalf: Be reconciled to God" (2 Corinthians 5:20).

That's our message. That's our calling. That's our sending. By God. For God. With God.

Rev. Dr. Gerald B. (Jerry) Kieschnick, President Emeritus, The Lutheran Church—Missouri Synod, former Texas District President and Former Chairman of the International Lutheran Council

COMPEL THE PEOPLE TO COME IN

Not so many years ago, a seminary graduate was sent to a congregation in a tough neighborhood in one of America's largest cities. He and a member of the congregation regularly took prayer walks in the church's neighborhood, praying for all who lived there. On one walk, they got into a conversation with a prostitute. The pastor offered her a copy of *Portals of Prayer* in an act of witness. She declined. The pastor persisted and offered the booklet to her again. She said, "I already have it," and she opened her purse and showed him the most recent edition.

Pause and think that through.

The *Missio Dei* came through the prayer walkers to a person who knew the Gospel but was still trapped by sin. How often do you and I get out of our congregations and into our communities where opportunities abound for real life-and-death witness?

"Go out to the highways and hedges and compel people to come in, that my house may be filled," writes Luke in chapter fourteen (v. 33) of his gospel.

For centuries, the Age of Reason dominated our western civilization. In its most extreme expression, reason was magisterial, all-judging, going so far as to reject faith and religion based upon revelation. This was the prevailing context in which the doctrinally strong Lutheran Church—Missouri Synod used reason ministerially, subservient to the revelation of God's Word. Hence our forebearers wisely insisted on well-educated clergy and church workers and developed colleges and a strong system of parochial schools.

Laity were taught the faith for head and heart, and apologetics used reason to witness the Christian revelation to those outside the Church. In our lifetimes the Age of Reason has given way to post-modernism. Today many parishioners, clergy, and church leaders are befuddled by a public culture that doesn't accept absolute truth, a society wherein the church no longer has special privilege, and where congregational life often seems to have lost its energy for gathering and outreach.

This much-needed volume takes us to God's inexhaustible source for faith and guidance, the living voice of the Gospel in God's Word. How can you and I experience the Word burning in our hearts as our Lord guides us in these new times? What will make Bible study so relevant that we can't wait to sit at our Lord's feet and learn? The prayer walkers demonstrate how: out of the sanctuary into the streets, out of our comfort zones and into community, out of our affinity groups to meet people who are perishing without Jesus.

Our Lutheran fathers attest "this fundamental and immovable fact, that the worship which is pleasing to God, internally and externally, both in our spiritual and outward life, is summed up in the Decalog. In the Second Table not even one word calls attention to the solitary life," writes Martin Chemnitz.

Philip Melanchthon adds: "The works of the Second Table are truly the worship of God."

And when the *Missio Dei* impels us to meet people still enslaved in sin, our empathy for them and our own cries for understanding return us again and again *ad fontes* (back to the sources), to Scripture and study, to worship with the Body of Christ, where we see anew, or maybe for the first time, that the *Missio Dei* to the world is still passionately coming to you and me. How will we hope to share it if we don't see ourselves how desperately we need it?

Rev. Dr. Dale Meyer, President Emeritus Concordia Seminary, St. Louis, former Lutheran Hour speaker and former Vice-President of the Lutheran Church—Missouri Synod

MORE THAN A SUPPORTING ROLE

It's time that God's Mission, often referred to as the *Missio Dei*, plays more than an adjunct or supporting role in the theology and practice of our Christian churches. The *Missio Dei* needs to stand at the heart and center of who we are as Christians and what we confess as God's true word or message to the world. As that center, the *Missio Dei* rightly serves as the principle hermeneutical lens through which we read the Scriptures and apply its message to ourselves and our world. In short, the *Missio Dei* determines the substance and shape of our being and purpose as a Christian church and our biblical confession to the world.

Fixing the *Missio Dei* as the center of our Biblical hermeneutics will seem audacious to some. We could not be so bold in making such an assertion unless the Scriptures themselves compelled us to do so.

And in fact, they do. In what I consider the most significant book written on the *Missio Dei* since David J. Bosch's comprehensive work, *Transforming Mission: Paradigm Shifts in the Theology of Mission* (Orbis Books: Maryknoll, NY, 1991), Christopher J. H. Wright argues that our Lord Himself identified His Mission as the hermeneutical key that unlocks the treasures of Old and New Testaments (*The Mission of God: Unlocking the Bible's Grand Narrative*. InterVarsity Press, Downers Grove, IL: 2006).

St. Luke records:

> Then he said to them, "These are my words that I spoke to you while I was still with you, that everything written about me in the Law of Moses and the Prophets and the

Psalms must be fulfilled." Then he opened their minds to understand the Scriptures, and said to them, "Thus it is written, that the Christ should suffer and on the third day rise from the dead, and that repentance to the forgiveness of sins should be proclaimed in his name to all nations, beginning from Jerusalem. You are witnesses of these things (Chapter 24, vs. 44-48).

Wright explains, "Luke tells us that with these words 'Jesus opened their minds so they could understand the Scriptures,' or, as we might put it, he was setting their hermeneutical orientation and agenda. The proper way for disciples of the crucified and risen Jesus to read their Scriptures is messianically and missionally" (page 30).

As Lutherans it is appropriate to push Wright's conclusion even further, acknowledging that we cannot read the Scriptures messianically unless we read them missionally. For in God's mind, the Author of Holy Writ, the two are inseparable. Christ's mission to save the world (John 3:16-17) is the sum and substance of His messianic anointing. Jesus made it perfectly clear to his hearers: You cannot embrace Me as Messiah without embracing My universal mission.

This inseparable connection between Messiah and mission was the very stone on which Christ's people stumbled (Luke 4). They wanted Jesus as their personal Messiah, but they rejected His messianic mission to the nations. Rejecting His mission led, finally, to rejecting Him as the Messiah. As a result, the Kingdom of God was taken from them and given to a people producing its fruits (Matthew 21).

Mark these words: Jesus's messianic mission, the stone upon

which His people stumbled, is the very stone upon which He builds His Church. Thus, St. Peter's Confession, "Thou art the Christ," must be grasped with a missional heart, if it is to be grasped at all.

The hermeneutical significance of the *Missio Dei* is likewise required for a proper reading of the Lutheran Confessions. How does such a claim square with what we confessionally hold as our Material Principle, justification by grace through faith alone? Again, they are inseparable.

Our Confessional center, justification by grace through faith, rests entirely on the Mission of God. In the 1991 Commission on Theology and Church Relations (CTCR) document, *A Theological Statement of Mission,* the *Missio Dei* is organized around the chief articles of faith – God, Original Sin, the Son of God, Justification, and the Ministry of the Church. The Father sent His Son into the world (John 3:17) to make perfect satisfaction for our sins through His death. We are declared righteous by God as a gift through faith when we believe that our sins are forgiven for Christ's sake.

Furthermore, the Father and the Son send the Holy Spirit into the world to create saving faith where and when it pleases Him. As our church fathers insisted, the Holy Spirit does not simply float out in space somewhere but anchors Himself to the Gospel as it is preached throughout the world. "So faith comes from hearing and hearing through the word (preaching) of Christ" (Romans 10).

What naturally and necessarily arise from our Lutheran confession of justification by grace through faith are St. Paul's great missionary questions: "But how are they to call on him in whom they have not believed? And how are they to believe in him of whom they have never heard? And how are they to hear without someone preaching? And how are they to preach unless they are sent?" (Romans 10).

We need to ask these questions afresh in our own time.

It is the *Missio Dei*—including the source and extent of its activity—that distinguishes Lutherans from other reformers on the matter of justification. Distinct from Anabaptists, we hold that God alone acts in our justification (divine monergism). He came to us, He died in our place, His Spirit works faith in our hearts through His external Word and Sacrament. We cling to the confidence that our righteousness is alien to us, a pure gift of God, without our energy or work. At the same time, our teaching of justification clings to the universal dimension of God's Mission: "[God our savior] desires all people to be saved and to come to the knowledge of the truth" (1 Timothy 2:4).

We distinguish ourselves from those Christians whose theological hermeneutic forces them to limit the scope of those whom God declares righteous for Christ's sake. We cling to the universality of God's grace in Christ. We evangelically ask the dual questions, "How can you and I be sure that God justified us if He did not justify all people everywhere in Christ (2 Timothy 3)? and, How can you and I be sure that our faith holds a sufficient or saving grasp on the righteousness of God if it is a product of our own human pursuit and sincerity?"

Can you imagine what would happen to our doctrine of justification by grace through faith if it did not assume the missional character and work of God who loved the world so much that He pursued (and still pursues) it in His Son Jesus Christ? Our faith stands solely and securely on these two missional assumptions— God alone and God for all. These missional assumptions form the bedrock upon which our Lutheran doctrine of justification stands firm.

The necessity of our returning to a missional hermeneutic has never been more critical than now. In our recently passed (and for some still passing) "churched-culture" era, pastors and congregations depended on the assumption that people might show up at church on their own volition. We based this assumption on the notion that American culture in general shared the value with the Church that Christian worship is a basic building block of our life and society. Nonbelievers are drawn to worship by the "natural law" operating in creation "that [all mankind] should seek after God in the hope that they might… find him" (Acts 17). While our U.S. Constitution is deliberate not to promote any religion over another, our American culture still gave the Christian church a virtual monopoly on the "seeking-after-God" options. Other world religions and religious options were simply not on the spiritual radar screens of most Americans. In that arena we Lutherans did not have to give significant consideration to the missional nature of our confessional theology. We could operate quite successfully as the confessional voice within the Christian church and the so-called "churched culture," attracting otherwise Christian-leaning folk to the pure Gospel.

Yet, as most (if not all) of us North American Christians would agree, those days have fled or are fleeing. We in the LCMS are painfully coming to grips with the fact that Christianity is no longer in the religious driver seat of our culture; instead, religious pluralism is. Our American culture no longer points people to the Christian church to find the answers to their spiritual questions, longings or basic values. It is neutral at best, even antagonistic, to the church's claim that she is the keeper of God's objective truth.

It questions the notion that there is even such a thing as objective truth.

In such an arena we should not be disappointed to find that people no longer look to the Christian church or her Lord in their spiritual meanderings. As Christians, we should not be surprised. Our Confessions teach plainly what the true nature of man is: "unable by nature to have true fear of God and true faith in God."

If there is any seeking and finding to be done, it is God alone who must do it. More than ever, now is the time for the *Missio Dei* to frame and interpret what we believe, teach, confess, and live.

Rev. Dr. Robert Newton, former President, California-Nevada-Hawaii District and former Professor of World Missions, Concordia Theological Seminary, Ft. Wayne

MISSIO DEI – WHAT *IS* THIS THING?

As it snows outside I'm contemplating Luke's account of Jesus's birth that will soon be read at Christmas Eve services. It's intriguing to consider the angelic announcement of "good news of great joy that will be for all people" (Luke 2:10) to the shepherds, the shepherds' unhesitating reaction to go to Bethlehem and see "this thing" (v. 15), with the immediate result that they made known the statement of the angels to others.

Even today as people listen to and encounter the truth of God's Word and will, the Holy Spirit mightily works, allowing them to see and believe "this thing" – God's goodness, His grace, mercy, and love – so that they experience his transformative power. Then, they too — almost immediately and inevitably — desire to make known the "good news of great joy."

What is this good news? That there is salvation, deliverance from missing the mark, deliverance from guilt and brokenness, and even death. Knowing and experiencing God and *deliberately sharing* the good news of a great joy — the very mission of God (*Missio Dei*) — go hand in hand. This coupling of salvation and deliverance occurred continually in the ministry of Jesus, as related in the Gospels. The healing of the demoniac and the Samaritan women at the well are two examples.

The salvation-deliverance pattern repeats itself—in almost uninterrupted fashion—in the Book of Acts. In Michael Green's *Evangelism in the Early Church,* the reader is taken through the Book of Acts and beyond to see how the Church – God's people – in the first 200 years after Pentecost lived as the salt of the earth and the light of the world and *prioritized* the sharing of the

Gospel (*"the word of the Lord continues to grow"*) in a hostile world. "Christians" recognized themselves as "nobodies" and yet simultaneously as "missionaries." "... neither the strategy nor the tactics of the first Christians were particularly remarkable," Green writes. "What was remarkable was their **conviction**, their **passion** and their **determination** to act as Christ's embassy to a rebel world, whatever the consequences."

These Christians embraced the fact that God's mission had a Church, not that the Church had a mission. Indeed, their ecclesiology, but especially their missiology, changed the world.

I pray that as Christ's embassy to a hostile world today we boldly do the same under the grace of God and in His strength!

The essays you will find in this volume are invitations for you to "rest," to be renewed in a relationship with God, and to be recentered and reacquainted with the *Missio Dei* – the Mission of God. This is the *Missio Dei:* a lively, purposeful recognition of God's sending and our going to the world.

Rev Dr. David P. E. Maier, President of the Michigan District of the Lutheran Church—Missouri Synod, Chairman of the LCMS Council of Presidents

INTRODUCTION

An open-heart five-bypass surgery is intense and invasive. Five blockages in the heart call for urgent attention and a physical heart transformation.

Spiritual blockage of the heart is just as serious, and we see it everywhere today – in strangers, in people who are close to us, and in the church as we know it. Our spiritual blockages call for urgent attention and a heart transformation. How? By a *Missio Dei* immersion. *Missio Dei* is Latin for "the sending of God." The *Missio Dei*, the sending of God, is Gospel!

The disciples in the first century AD excelled in the multiplication and growth of the Word, as recorded in the Book of Acts. By contrast, the church in the twenty-first century appears to be evading Christ's sending, experiencing decline rather than growth. Today's church is short of breath, too weak to move out of its comfort zone of preoccupation with itself, and too complacent to venture into evangelical territory while continuing to strive for its purity of doctrine. Programs don't work. Old mindsets and habits prevail. The church as we know it today is dying missionally, drowning in indolence and apathy. It is therefore in urgent need of an intense and invasive treatment: a deep dive into God's Word.

A consortium of well-known missional leaders in The Lutheran Church—Missouri Synod (LCMS) invite and challenge every Christian individual, congregation, and organization to participate in a *Missio Dei* Jubilee Immersion. The term "Jubilee" is a festival year (period or event) of redemption, renewal, and reset based on God's provision in the Old Testament. This Biblical immersion is driven by three main purposes:

1. Encouraging Christ-believers to immerse themselves in the Gospel, understand God's word more thoroughly and thereby participate in God's Great Sending

2. A surge in pastors, church workers, and congregations who come to know, understand, and apply the *Missio Dei*, the Great Sending of God in Christ

3. A movement of heart transformations and commitments to immerse in the Missio Dei, inspired and guided by 2 Corinthians 5:14-15 – *For the love of Christ controls us, because we have concluded this: that one has died for all, therefore all have died; and he died for all, that those who live might no longer live for themselves but for him who for their sake died and was raised;* and 1 John 3:16 – *By this we know love, that he laid down his life for us, and we ought to lay down our lives for the brothers.*

With confidence in Christ, may the exercise of his Word and the power of the Holy Spirit give birth to a mended heart renewed by a Missio Dei spirit and mindset!

The Jubilee Missio Dei Immersion includes:

- 42 *Missio Dei* scriptural texts, introduced by commentaries from a consortium of Christ-missional leaders

- a scriptural digest that explains the sending motif of John 17:18 and 20:21-23 in the context of John's Gospel proclaiming God as a sending God

- a *Missio Dei* Catechism to encourage intense ongoing scriptural study, based on history that demonstrates catechesis as an effective teaching tool

This Jubilee Immersion is not intended for the growth of any one institutional church or denomination, such as the LCMS, but rather for the growth of the Kingdom of Christ, to spread God's glory, to rescue souls and bring them salvation.

Since God, by His Word, made us in His image (Genesis 1:27), this initiative urges a total immersion in the Word of God. This Great Sending is not meant to be a piece-meal or periodic heart treatment. Instead, it is an all-consuming scriptural and Gospel focus on the sending of God. It is a spiritually radical heart surgery, a life-changing immersion in the Word for a missional heart transformation. Come along on a jubilee re-set and life-changing immersion in the *Missio Dei*, the Great Sending, God's heart for the world beating through you.

LEADER'S GUIDE

INTRODUCTION

For a *Missio Dei* Immersion to be successful, it is important that all participants first have a thorough understanding of what a *Missio Dei* Immersion is. Helping participants understand the multifaceted concept, its benefits and its urgency is the pastor's (or leader's) job.

The Scriptural *Missio Dei* Immersion is an intense and prolonged study of Scripture examining the sending nature of God through Bible studies, sermon series, God's means of grace, and commentaries, prayers, and resources provided by former LCMS District Presidents, former Synod Vice-Presidents, and a former Synod President.

But if participants in this Great Sending are to undergo a true heart transformation, it is critical that they develop a thorough understanding of what a Biblically inspired immersion is, its means of implementation, benefits, and urgency.

Paul writes in Romans 12:1-2, "I appeal to you therefore, brothers, by the mercies of God, to present your bodies as a living sacrifice, holy and acceptable to God, which is your spiritual worship. Do not be conformed to this world, but be transformed by the renewal of your mind, that by testing you may discern what is the will of God, what is good and acceptable and perfect."

Here Paul describes an intensive mind-renewal and discernment as urged by God. This passage can be appropriately interpreted as a call for all of God's people – pastors, congregations and individuals – to undergo a radical heart transformation, submitting to God's will for participating in His mission. By immersing ourselves in God's Missio Dei Gospel ("Missio Dei" is Latin for "the sending of God") we offer a living and holy, acceptable sacrifice. Taking the time to understand God's sending mission is an ongoing act of spiritual worship by transformation, renewal, examination, and discernment of God's good and perfect will.

The only way to encounter a true heart transformation as God describes through Paul is through a Scriptural immersion, or an intense prolonged study involving deep dives into Scripture, sermon series, leadership seminars, commentaries, prayers, and resources such as those provided in this publication.

This Great Sending of God immersion is ground-breaking. It asks that pastors and congregation members take a long and significant break from the normal activities and routines of congregational life. It urges participants to put the brakes on business as usual and re-examine their understanding of God, how God works and what he asks of us. This spiritual break of routine is supported in Scripture with concepts such as "Jubilee" (a re-set, re-turn, and redemption year) and "Sabbath" (a rest and renewal) and via the number "40" (where we see in numerous settings intense and fixed reflection).

See additional rationale for a jubilee immersion under missiological resources for The Great Sending.

BIBLICAL IMMERSION PATTERNS

1. "40" – Patterned after the biblical significance of the number "40." The number appears again and again in Scripture. For example:

a. Israel wandered for 40 years in the wilderness

b. Moses spent 40 days on Mount Sinai

c. Nineveh was given 40 days' respite

d. Spies spent 40 days in Canaan

e. God flooded the earth with 40 days of rain

f. Jesus fasted for 40 days

g. The season of Lent lasts 40-days

h. Ascension Day is celebrated 40 days after Christ's Resurrection

2. Emphasis on the biblical concepts of "Sabbath" and "Jubilee"– a concentrated period of reset, rest, reflection, and renewal with the Lord, away from the routine, the old habits, the usual parish duties, and programs. (God spent the seventh day of creation resting with Adam and Eve in holy contemplation.) Consider:

a. If a pastor/professor is encouraged to take a sabbatical, certainly a congregation can break the routine, dismiss, or break any unproductive habits or events, and execute a concentrated Scriptural immersion in the *Missio Dei*, the Great Sending, as a congregational sabbatical with the pastor.

b. If a wheat farmer recognizes the benefit of and practices a crop fallow (land laying unseeded for a considerable time, for restoration), the conditions in our world are ripe for a Jubilee *Missio Dei* Immersion.

c. That God planned for a Jubilee year, the Year of the Lord's Favor (see Leviticus 25; Isaiah 58:5; 61:1-2;

and Luke 4:18-19) for a reset, a time of rest. "Rest," in the context that God meant it, was a time of restoration or caring for the land, returning property to its original owner, and freeing the Israelite slaves.

The Hebrew word for "jubilee" is "yowbel," which translates literally as "ram's horn trumpet." Therefore, a pastor and congregation can mark a Mission Jubilee Immersion with the joyful blast of a trumpet, to mark an important day of the Lord. Consider this Word of God-trumpet blast as an official kickoff of a *Missio Dei* Immersion initiative. The Immersion might focus on:

i.   a return to the original, or a return to the "property" (the ground, or reason) of the church's existence

ii. a returning of the "property" to the *Missio Dei* focus, which belongs to God; or

iii. a reset to Christ's mission of redemption to free all slaves (sinners) from sin, including sins of apathy and of not focusing on nor having the mindset of Christ to "seek and save the lost" (Luke 19:10)

THE JUBILEE YEAR SUGGESTED IMPLEMENTATION FORMATS

A consecutive period of 40 + 2 (2 additional for good measure, pressed down and running over) Bible studies and sermon series texts. The 42-consecutive period may take on one of the following formats, organized here from the most beneficial to the least intense:

a. One Jubilee Year of 42 consecutive weeks, with one Bible study immersion (lesson) per week. This leaves the remaining 10 weeks of the year open to other considerations of the church calendar or additional immersion Bible studies determined and provided by the pastor. Suggested format: A yearlong *Missio Dei* Immersion can begin on January 1st or the Sunday after Easter, whatever is determined best by the participating pastor and congregation. This is considered the greatest benefit

b. 3 seven-week periods per year, over two years. *Suggested format:* One Bible study immersion (lesson) per week for seven weeks, for a total of 21 immersions (three modules per year) for 2 consecutive Jubilee years. Example: One module in the fall incorporating Advent and one or two in the Winter/Spring incorporating Lent

c. 2 seven-week periods per year, over three years. *Suggested format:* One Bible study immersion (lesson) per week for seven weeks, for a total of 14 immersions (two modules per year) for 3 consecutive Jubilee years. Example: One module in the fall incorporating Advent and one in the Winter/Spring incorporating Lent

d. 42 days over one six-week period for the year, one module per week with one *Missio Dei* lesson per day

e. (An alternative is to add another 7 days for a total of 7 weeks (49 days), instead of 6 weeks, with the local pastor determining the additional 7 immersion Bible studies).

f. The *Theological Basis for the Great Sending in John's Gospel* and the *Missio Dei Catechism* can serve as additional teaching/training tools throughout the 6 (or 7) weeks, the given year, or for years ahead.

g. Any other adaptation of the 42-consecutive period as deemed appropriate by the local pastor and congregational leaders

The *Missio Dei* Word of God Immersion must be coordinated and intentional:

a. with worship services, readings, sermons, hymns, and prayers associated with it

b. with a mission-focused Sunday School curriculum

c. with the engagement of each member (thus practicing being a sent one, sent to one another)

    i. in the 42 Bible studies and accompanying commentaries (personal and/or group participation)

    ii. in regularly scheduled *Missio Dei* catechesis (adults and youth)

    iii. in writing and sharing prayers. Prayers are provided for each immersion day. Pastors, congregational leaders, and lay members (including children) are encouraged to write, speak, and share the prayers with one another.

    iv. in writing and sharing testimonies. Pastors, congregational leaders, and lay members (including children) are encouraged to share favorite Bible passages and what embracing Christ and His mission means to them. Consider incorporating one lay testimony per immersion day.

e. with workshops led by pastors and lay leaders using the Bible Studies, the Sending Digest, and the *Missio Dei* Catechism

f. with suggested self-study tools available from one's church body or other mission entity to test and examine the mission and ministry of the congregation

g. with study and meditation on the Twelve Mission Theses (see Chapter 7), leading to a *Missio Dei* commitment, conviction, and confession (Recall Luther's famous words, "Here I stand")

h. with regular and ongoing communication via social media, email, and text messaging, according to participants' preferred communication methods

THE URGENCY OF THE HEART TRANSFORMATION AND BECOMING IMMERSED IN THE GREAT SENDING

A Jubilee immersion is urgent because the *Sending God (Missio Dei),* which is the central nature and activity of God, is the core teaching of Scripture. The *Missio Dei* is not a branch of Christian doctrine or faith. Rather, it is the core, the very heart and center, of Christian doctrine *and* faith. It is not an adjunct or appendage. We are considering how our missional God made us and calls us to be a part of his great sending. A central question is, will every person who embraces Christ and his rescue embrace his mission? Will every Christ-believer be Christ's missionary, as God intends?

And that leads to another key question: will every congregation be a church in Christ's mission, a missionary church, a *Missio Dei* church (one holy Christian apostolic church), wholly participating in the Great Sending?

The Great Sending is not just another start-and-stop program or a quick-fix. It is not simply a one-and-done activity, nor a duty among and equal to other routine parish duties. The execution of the Great Sending requires a mending (Matthew 4:21), a perfecting (Ephesians 4:12), a restoration (2 Corinthians 13:9), an adjustment or equipping (Hebrews 13:21). The Biblical Greek word used in these texts is καταρτίζω (katartizō), which means to *complete thoroughly, repair* or *adjust,* mend, make perfect, prepare, reset, restore. The Greek word has the presumption of brokenness, disconnectedness, deformity, being torn, imperfect, incomplete, not fully fit. The word would be appropriate to describe an orthopedic surgeon resetting broken bones, or a fisherman mending torn nets.

This Biblical depiction is exactly why a scriptural *Missio Dei* Immersion is necessary. This is a matter of an urgent heart transformation, a Biblical jubilee reset!

PARTICIPANTS' STUDY GUIDE

INTRODUCTION

Sanctify them in the truth; your word is truth. As you sent me into the world, so I have sent them into the world. And for their sake I consecrate myself, that they also may be sanctified in truth.

—John 17:17-19

Transformation does not happen automatically or by coincidence. It is only the powerful Word of God and his Gospel that produces fruit and that changes hearts. Embracing Christ and His mission is more than a cursory or superficial treatment of God's Word. It means diving deep and diligently into God's Word, to not only know God's will but to understand His will in depth and apply it accordingly. *God stresses this truth in Deuteronomy 6:6-9:* And these words that I command you today shall be on your heart. You shall *teach them diligently* to your children and shall *talk of them when you sit in your house*, and when you *walk by the way*, and *when you lie down*, and *when you rise*. You shall *bind them* as a sign on your hand, and they shall be as *frontlets between your eyes*. You shall *write them* on the doorposts of your house and on your gates" (emphasis mine).

God's word is powerful. Any student immersed in the Bible will treasure, reflect on, and fix in memory God's truth, again and again. He/she will, as the "Collect for the Word" says, "hear... read, mark, learn, and inwardly digest..." (*The Lutheran Hymnal*, "The Order of Morning Service," page 14). We are powerless to transform our own hearts. But God in His Word can boldly change, transform, and lead us, including in this Word-of-God encounter, to powerful and meaningful immersion in his *Missio Dei*, which is the Gospel core.

See *additional rationale for a jubilee immersion under missiological resources for* The Great Sending.

THE STUDY GUIDE

A key feature of the Jubilee *Missio Dei* Immersion is the series of 42 Bible studies and sermon series texts, each introduced with a commentary and discussion questions by a theologically trained and Christ-missional-minded leader. The following study guide suggests how Immersion participants seeking a shift in thought and behavior (repentance) – a heart transformation – can benefit the most from each of the 42 Bible study segments. Whether studying personally or in a group, utilize this study guide for each of the 42 Bible study segments, which demonstrate the pattern of preparation, study, reflection, and application. Under this pattern, this study can be done as an individual or in groups.

- Begin with a prayer for a sanctified heart transformation in the truth of the Word
- Read and digest each passage
  o Repeat in your own words what each text says
- Read, digest, and discuss the commentary and questions provided by missional-minded leaders
  o Think of the commentaries and questions as the

"appetizers" for each immersion. Consider using them as devotional introductions or study aides to help you get more out of the biblical texts

o Read the commentary a second and third time to grasp it thoroughly

- Use the commentaries, individual study, and discussion with others to seek meaning of and deeper insight into each biblical text

o Take time to comprehend how all the pieces fit together

- Explore questions to deepen engagement in the mission focus

o Ask yourself and each other questions

o Don't be afraid to be curious – no question is a dumb question

- Pray for wisdom to apply the texts to yourself and your congregation

o Share your perspective. How do you see the texts applying to God's will and life's situations?

- Discuss and determine specific practices or courses of action, based on your studies of the texts

o Apply the text to regular practices and behavior

- Review yours and your congregation's existing practices and activities to test how they align to the *Missio Dei* (see Romans 12:1-3)

- Based on yours and others' insights, what specific changes would you suggest, for yourself and/or your congregation?

- o Ask yourselves where you need to repent (change your thinking and behavior)
- How will these studies spur you to participate more fully in Christ's mission from now on?
  - o Through prayer and reflection, determine your own fruits of repentance
- Close in the same way you began, with prayer
  - o Pray for a sanctified heart transformation to become immersed in the *Missio Dei*

The awesome genius of God's grace is that God gives us what He requires of us. We need salvation and He provided it through His Son. Saving faith in Christ is required to receive His gift of salvation, and He creates and gives us that saving faith. A living relationship with Christ is required for us to grow in love and knowledge of God, and God the Holy Spirit creates and offers us that relationship through His means of grace. A sanctified life is required to honor God, and the holiness of Christ is provided through the sanctifying power of the Holy Spirit. Loving God and each other with all our hearts, minds, and souls is required by God to make and strengthen disciples. He provides that love through the Gospel power of His own love and forgiveness. The Great Sending is Gospel-centered. The sending of God, the *Missio Dei*, is Gospel, giving what God requires, including participation in God's sending, God's heart for the world beating through you.

The Triune God, who has created, redeemed, chosen, called, and gathered us, also creates and transforms the missional heart through the penetrating power of his Word. The commentators for the *Missio Dei* Immersion Bible studies are God's representatives, sent to serve the church-at-large by bringing the power of God's Word to each participant in the Immersion. These commentators, all of whom possess *Missio Dei* hearts, have generously provided the Bible studies for use in the greater overall Immersion.

The motivation, conviction, and passion for the *Missio Dei* is found in God's Word. The driving forces behind the *Missio Dei* Immersion do not come from the works, practices, activities, and performances of missions. Through His Word, God creates a *Missio Dei* person and congregation –the core of who we are. The knowledge, understanding, and wisdom of the *Missio Dei* can only come from God, who we encounter and come to know through Scripture.

In the sending of the apostles, as recorded in Christ's high priestly prayer in John 17, Christ supplied the apostles with the sanctifying power of the Word of truth. So also, God's grace will provide us with the sanctifying power in the Jubilee Mission Immersion. Christ's prayer for the early apostles is also his prayer for us: "Sanctify them in the truth; your word is truth. As you sent me into the world, so I have sent them into the world. And for their sake I consecrate myself, that they also may be sanctified in truth."

According to *A Theological Statement of Mission*, published in 1991 by the LCMS's Commission on Theology and Church Relations, "Mission begins in the heart of God and expresses His great love for the world. It is the Lord's gracious initiative and ongoing activity to save a world incapable of saving itself... The mission will end as it began, in the heart of God."

As mission begins in the heart of God, our participation in His mission begins in our own hearts. God's sending mission is rooted in a Jubilee Immersion, an extensive opportunity for pastors and congregations to immerse themselves in God's Word, come to thoroughly know Christ's sending mission, and encounter a *Missio Dei* heart transformation and mind-reset.

> *Remember not the former things, nor consider the things of old. Behold, I am doing a new thing; now it springs forth, do you not perceive it? I will make a way in the wilderness and rivers in the desert.*
>
> —Isaiah 43:18-19

> *And I will give you a new heart, and a new spirit I will put within you. And I will remove the heart of stone from your flesh and give you a heart of flesh.*
>
> —Ezekiel 36:26

BIBLE STUDIES FOR
THE GREAT SENDING

CHAPTER 1

CHRIST IS THE HEART OF THE GREAT SENDING

STUDY 1: The Sending Christ

John 20

Rev. Dr. Dean Nadasdy

> *Jesus said to them again, "Peace be with you. As the Father has sent me, even so I am sending you."*
>
> —John 20:21

COMMENTARY

The mission of God needs a risen Christ, not a dead king who went out in a flame of glory as a martyr on a cross. The evangelist John, an eyewitness to Christ's ministry, gives us what we need. He remembers the sprint to the tomb with Peter. Seemingly ever competitive, he remembers that he got there first. Peter goes in. John follows. They see only Jesus' burial cloths. John writes of himself at that moment, "He [I] saw and believed" (John 20:8).

Peter and John saw a tomb without a body and still had much to learn. In a tender encounter after they leave, though, Mary actually sees the risen Lord. He calls her by name and says He is ready to ascend to His Father. Mary tells the disciples, "I have seen the Lord" (John 20:18).

In the blazing light of the resurrection and the reality of Jesus' immanent return to the Father, the mission of God needs something else – a sending. Those who see the risen Christ must be sent, and not just by anyone. They must be sent by Him. This is His mission. Those who see the risen Christ must not speak on their own authority, but on His. They must not depend on themselves or on one another, but on Him. So, on Easter night, the risen Christ appears behind locked doors to speak an understated common blessing to His frightened, cloistered disciples: "Peace be with you." He shows them His crucifixion wounds. The disciples' fear melts away in the gladness of seeing Jesus alive. (See John 20:19-23.)

With no small talk (at least none recorded) in that locked room, Jesus turns to the business of sending. "As the Father has sent me," he says, "even so I am sending you" (John 20:21). John recalls Jesus breathing on those ten disciples. Perhaps this was a sign of the promised Holy Spirit. Perhaps it was His life-giving breath for the mission ahead. With that breath of life, though, Christ gives them what they need for their mission – the promise of the Spirit and the authority to forgive and to retain sins. Eight days later, in an act of extraordinary, individualized grace, He would come back for Thomas, who was absent on that first night.

Jesus never envisioned a church kept in hiding behind locked doors, concerned for its institutional health and survival. He sends His followers into the world. To be sent by Christ is to share in the very same mission on which the Father had sent His son – the forgiveness of sins. That mission extends to the neighbor next door and to the neighbor on another continent. Only the One who went through the dying and came back alive could do this sending.

A young missionary, fresh from the seminary, was being introduced to a village of indigenous people by the missionary he would replace. The new arrival responded to his introduction by saying: "In the wisdom of God and in accordance with the proper procedures of the church, following my matriculation with a Master of Sacred Theology degree and ordination into the holy ministry, I stand before you as a humble steward of the mysteries of God, announcing the sacred kerygma of Christ."

The chief of the village looked quizzically at the old missionary as if to ask, "What did he just say?" The wise veteran of years of service in the mission field simply smiled and said, "This young man wants you to know that Jesus sent him here to your village with some really good news."

It matters where we come from. To be sent means we come from the One with nail prints on His hands and feet, the One forever breathing life into His church and its witness.

DISCUSSION QUESTIONS

1. How "sent by Christ" do you feel? That is, how aware are you each day that Christ has sent you on His mission to proclaim the forgiveness of sins?

2. What does it mean to you that the risen Christ came back for Thomas? What does this say about Jesus, about

Thomas, about you?

3. As a mission-hearted Christian, give your best answer to the question, "Where do you come from?"

PRAYER

Send me, Lord Jesus. Bring peace to my heart. Breathe life into my witness. Help me to speak and live as one both humbled and emboldened under Your authority. Send your church, Lord. Challenge us. Shake us up. Send us on a mission that can only be engaged because You are the One sending us. For Your name's sake. Amen.

STUDY 2: Who do People Say Jesus Is?
Matthew 16:13-20

Rev. Dr. Larry Stoterau

Now when Jesus came into the district of Caesarea Philippi, he asked his disciples, "Who do people say that the Son of Man is?"

—Matthew 16:13

He said to them, "But who do you say that I am?"

—Matthew 16:15

COMMENTARY

"Who are you?"

This is one of the fundamental questions of those who challenged Jesus.

From the scribes and Pharisees who were threatened by His claims of being the "Son of God" to Pilate's question, "Are you the King of the Jews?" (Matthew 27:11) people failed to understand Christ's purpose and His message.

For those who do not believe, the question remains the same today. The message of the *Missio Dei* is to introduce Jesus Christ, the Son of the Living God, to those who do not yet know Him.

In Matthew 16:13-20, Jesus asks his disciples, "Who do people say the Son of Man is?"

The disciples are quick to answer with the names they have heard: John the Baptist, Elijah, Jeremiah, or one of the prophets. Their answers are not surprising, since the people well could have recalled the promises of a future messenger in the Old Testament. In Deuteronomy 18:15, Moses declares that God will raise up a new prophet who will lead the people. Malachi 3:1 promises One who will come and prepare the way, and Malachi 4:5-6 promises the sending of Elijah before the great and terrible day of the Lord.

Peter speaks for the group when he says that Jesus is "the Christ, the Son of the Living God" (Matthew 16:16). Jesus is quick to point out that this knowledge was revealed to Peter by God. Then Jesus commends Peter's faith, claiming he is no longer known as "Simon Bar Jonah" but as Peter. It is on this faith witnessed by Peter that Christ will build his church.

In his Gospel, Matthew is clear: Jesus is the Christ. From the sweeping genealogy in Chapter 1 to the testimony of John the Baptist in Chapter 11, to the testimony of Peter in our text, Jesus is "The Christ." It is not possible to know who Jesus is apart from understanding Him as "Messiah." "Messiah" stems from the Hebrew word, *Mashiach*, which means "the chosen one."

People may know the story of Christmas and even the story of Easter without recognizing that this Jesus is both God and man, the Chosen One to deliver us from sin through death and resurrection. Even Peter does not understand the work of Jesus (16:21-23) until he himself has been to the cross and has met the risen Messiah in the upper room.

Like Peter, we have been to the cross and have met the risen Lord. Only instead of meeting Him in a locked upper room, we meet Him in the Word and Sacraments. Because He comes to us, we are able to proclaim Jesus Christ as the Son of the Living God.

DISCUSSION QUESTIONS

1. Why is it significant for believers to know that Jesus is both fully human and fully divine?

2. If a friend were to ask you who Jesus is, how would you answer?

3. We rejoice that our God is a "living God" who is active in our lives. Where do you see Him at work in your life right now?

PRAYER

Dear Father in Heaven, I thank you for the gift of Your Son, Jesus, who gave His life for me. I rejoice in Your love and forgiveness and pray that I may be a bold witness of Your love to those who do not yet know Jesus. Grant us Your peace and joy in the name of Jesus, the Christ. Amen.

STUDY 3: Christ Crucified
John 18-19

Rev. Dr. Dean Nadasdy

> *So he delivered him over to them to be crucified. So they took Jesus, and he went out, bearing his own cross, to the place called The Place of a Skull, which in Aramaic is called Golgotha. There they crucified him, and with him two others, one on either side, and Jesus between them.*
>
> —John 19:16-18

COMMENTARY

A piece of ancient Roman graffiti depicts a Christian kneeling before a donkey-headed figure on a cross. The caption reads, "Alexamenos worships [his] god." The graffiti ridicules Christians who worship a convicted criminal dying on a cross. It is no wonder that artistic depictions of the crucified Christ in the early years of Christianity are rare. More likely to see was the figure of a young Apollo-like shepherd carrying a sheep on his shoulders or Jesus healing a crippled man. To preach (or depict) a crucified Christ was, as the apostle Paul put it, a "stumbling block" (*skandalon* in Greek) to Jews and "foolishness" (*moria* in Greek) to Greeks (1 Corinthians 1:23). It is hard to see victory in an execution.

Chapters 18-19 of John's Gospel give us the arrest, trials, crucifixion, and burial of Jesus Christ. For John the cross of Jesus Christ is anything but an embarrassment. John was there. He saw the arrest in the garden, the Sanhedrin trial, and the crucifixion. John's eyewitness account of these events does not present Jesus as a donkey on a cross. Building on Jesus' own words, John presents the crucifixion as a lifting up (3:14f), a glorification (8:28), and even an enthronement of the Messiah King (12:31-33).

Throughout His arrest, trial, and execution, Jesus seems to be totally in charge. He is declared a king by Pilate. In the Gospel of John, there is no Simon to help with the cross; Jesus bears it on His own. John includes no mockery of Jesus from under the cross or from those crucified with Him. Jesus shows no signs of being delirious on the cross. He takes care of those He loves. Fully conscious, He gives a cry of victory, "It is finished" (John 19:30). There is no darkness at Golgotha in John's record, only light.

The crucified Christ in John's Gospel willingly and authoritatively fulfills the mission given Him by the Father. There is no reason for embarrassment here for those who follow and proclaim Him. Jesus suffers on the cross, alright. His suffering is real. Yet in His suffering and in His dying, He is enthroned on the cross. This is the glory of which He spoke along the way. It is a glory further illuminated by His resurrection. There was no doubt in John's heart when he wrote in his prologue, "We have seen His glory…" (John 1:14).

In the mission of God, Christian witnesses will always lift high the cross of Jesus Christ as an ensign of victory. The cross is less of a scandal now. We wear crosses as jewelry. We hang crosses in our sanctuaries. There is, however, no denying its suffering and ignominy. Yet John's eyewitness record of the cross brings us another perspective, that of victory – the willing, authoritative sacrifice of the Son of God. His gospel enthrones Christ on the cross and proclaims Him *Christus Victor* over the forces of evil in the world.

In proclaiming Christ, those on His mission must be careful never to present the cross as defeat and the resurrection as victory. Christ is glorified in both; in both Christ is victorious.

DISCUSSION QUESTIONS

1. How do you think our culture sees the cross today?

2. How effective are we as witnesses in presenting the cross as a sign of victory rather than of defeat?

3. What does it mean to you to glory in the cross of Christ?

PRAYER

Lord Christ, You went headlong to the cross and claimed it as Your throne. As Your witnesses may we ever glory in Your cross, boldly proclaiming Your victory over sin, death, and the devil. Amen.

STUDY 4: A Christ for All Peoples

Luke 4:18-21; 23

Rev. Dr. Robert Newton

The Spirit of the Lord is upon me, because he has anointed me to proclaim good news to the poor. He has sent me to proclaim liberty to the captives and recovering of sight to the blind, to set at liberty those who are oppressed, to proclaim the year of the Lord's favor.

—Luke 4:18-19

Doubtless you will quote to me this proverb, "Physician, heal yourself." What we have heard you did at Capernaum, do here in your hometown as well.

—Luke 4:23

COMMENTARY

St. Luke takes us quickly from our Lord's confrontation with the evil one to His public appearance as a prophet in His hometown of Nazareth. Jesus had already been preaching and teaching in other synagogues in Galilee; however, it's in Nazareth – before His childhood friends and kinfolk – that He formally reveals Who He is and why He has come.

As St. Luke records later (Chapter 24), our Lord Jesus is the fulfillment of all that God had written in the Law of Moses, through the Prophets, and in the Psalms. So, Jesus turned to the Prophet Isaiah, the 61st chapter, to announce His mission. Multiple points are packed into these few verses, but here we will focus on three.

1. Jesus is the Christ, the *anointed* Messiah, promised from of old to God's people, Israel. He was anointed by His Father with the Holy Spirit in His baptism. He carries out His mission by and in the authority and power of the Holy Spirit.

2. His mission centers around the proclamation of the Good News from His Father. St. Luke describes Christ's ministry in a few ways. First, He ministers, literally, to good news people (εὐαγγελίσασθαι), or, as my good friend and colleague Dr. Eugene Bunkowske often said, His mission is "to gossip the Gospel." Obviously, a great deal of gossiping had already taken place prior to Jesus' arrival in His hometown. Luke tells us that "a report about him went out through all the surrounding country" (4:14). The other verb, kurusso (κηρύξαι), often translated as proclaim, herald, or preach, expresses more formal and official communication – a king's official messenger proclaiming a royal declaration to the king's subjects. It should give us great personal comfort to note who Isaiah identifies as the King's subjects: the poor, enslaved, blind, and oppressed. In short, His subjects are you and me. Whether formal or informal, the gracious words proclaimed by our Lord do exactly what His Father intends them to do – eternally bless the poor in spirit; set free those enslaved in sin; heal, both physically and spiritually, those who are blind; relieve those oppressed by the brokenness of this fallen creation; and rightly (justly) realign His creation to its divine and perfect order (a cosmic Shalom), just as the Year of Jubilee intended every fifty years for the nation of Israel.

3. Finally, Jesus tells us that He was specifically sent by His Father to accomplish these great deeds. The verb Isaiah uses to express this is apostello (ἀποστεῖλαι), from which we get the word "apostle" or "sent one." And like the verb kurusso above, apostello denotes an official sending, which includes the requisite authority needed to complete the specific assignment or mission. In this case, our Lord Jesus was sent by His Father not to condemn the world, but to save it (John 3:17).

Unfortunately, Jesus's understanding of His mission and its announcement ran counter to his friends' and family's expectations in Nazareth. They expected, perhaps even demanded, that He be their Messiah *exclusively*. In their minds, He owed them. Their sense of entitlement blinded them from seeing our Lord's divine calling: being *sent* by His Father to be Savior of the *world*. When Jesus reminded his friends and family members that the great prophets of old had been sent to bring God's favor not only to His people but also to the nations (including a widow from the Sidonian City of Zarephath and the lead general of the enemy army of Syria) they exploded with rage. The people of Nazareth labored vigorously to maintain their ceremonial purity – even down to the types of lamps and kitchen vessels they kept in their homes. They believed they deserved God's favor by their piety and their purity.

Yet the unclean Gentiles did not deserve God's blessing; they deserved only His wrath and judgement, as Isaiah stated in his prophecy, "the day of vengeance of our God" (61:2). (Interestingly, our Lord did not include those words of condemnation in His reading of the text.) Somehow and somewhere along the way

God's people had lost all sense of their Divine partnership – the covenant cut between them and their living God at Sinai (Exodus 19) – to be holy priests *for* the nations. Their penchant for personal purity blinded them to God's compassion for the world. Their myopic understanding of God's Kingdom, and, therefore, Christ's Mission, moved them to reject Jesus as their Messiah, and to their great loss. "And He did not do many mighty works there, because of their unbelief" (Matthew 13:58).

There is so much to learn from this text! As prophets like Isaiah had long promised, our Lord Jesus was *sent* by His Father to redeem and restore His people as His own. His people include you and me. His people include *vastly more* than you and me. His Divine mission encompasses the whole world. His own people, because of their self-righteous pursuit of personal and corporate purity from the world, found it impossible to embrace Him as God's chosen Messiah for the world, and as a result, precluded themselves from entering His Kingdom and its coming. Jesus' announcement of His mission in Nazareth and His people's reaction to it offer us a wonderful promise of grace and a dire warning against religious entitlement. As the poor, broken-hearted slaves to sin that we are, we need to hear His gracious words, which, when applied personally, sound like this: "My Father anointed and sent me to heal, forgive, release, and restore you." We also need to hear those words in the context of His missionary heart and mind: "And I have other sheep that are not of this fold. I must bring them also, and they will listen to my voice. So, there will be one flock, one shepherd" (John 10:16).

His public announcement invites all who have "ears to hear" (Matthew 11:15) to be reconciled to His Father by grace through faith alone and simultaneously to join Him in the mission upon which His Father sent Him – to unite all things (and all people) in heaven and on earth in perfect shalom under our Messianic King.

DISCUSSION QUESTIONS

1. The people of Nazareth thought they were entitled to receive Jesus' gracious Words and deeds because they were his friends and relatives. What things cause us to feel entitled to receive God's grace and mercy? How do we counteract this sense of entitlement?

2. Nazareth was a thoroughly Jewish community. As such, the people labored non-stop to keep themselves pure from the spiritual uncleanness of the Gentile world surrounding them. Their penchant for personal purity, however, blinded them to God's compassion for the world and their participation in His mission. We in the LCMS also have a penchant for purity; in this case, purity of doctrine. As essential as doctrinal purity is, when might our emphasis on it get in the way of our participation in God's mission to the world?

3. Our Lord once responded to those offended by His eating with sinners: "Go and learn what this means: 'I desire mercy, and not sacrifice.' For I came not to call the righteous, but sinners" (Matthew 9:13). Sacrifices were those things offered to God in praise, petition, and thanksgiving; mercy shows itself in the saving gifts of God we offer to the world in His Name. How do sacrifice and mercy apply to us today? Why does our Lord prefer mercy over sacrifice?

PRAYER

Dear Lord Jesus, Messiah of the nations, stir up in us hearts that cling to you and your grace alone. As your beloved people, open our eyes and hearts to see and respond with you to the brokenness of our world. Enable us to join you in the Mission upon which your Father has anointed and sent you. Anoint us with the same Holy Spirit, Who would empower and compel us to proclaim your saving Gospel to the ends of the earth. For your Name's sake. Amen.

STUDY 5: Jesus is the Son of God

John 1:29-34

Rev. Kenneth Hennings

And I have seen and have borne witness that this is the Son of God.
—John 1:34

COMMENTARY

John the Baptist plays a prominent part in the first chapter of the Gospel of John. There is a nice back-and-forth play between what is probably an early hymn of the church and John the Baptist, setting up his introduction of Jesus as the "Lamb of God" and "the Son of God."

In the other Gospels, Jesus is baptized by John the Baptist, the dove descends on Jesus, and the voice of God declares Jesus to be his Son whom he loves. In John's Gospel, John the Baptist recounts Jesus's baptism with the dove descending, but John the Baptist is the one who gives the witness that Jesus is "the Son of God."

John clearly wants to declare, from the beginning of his Gospel, who Jesus is and the purpose of Jesus' ministry. John points to Jesus as "the Son of God" from the creation of the world and identifies His ministry purpose as "the Lamb of God who takes away the sin of the world" (John 1:29). The "Lamb of God" is only used twice in the New Testament, both in John Chapter 1. Through these two terms ("Son of God" and "Lamb of God"),

John tells us what the "*Missio Dei*" (the mission of God) is – the forgiveness of sins through the life, death, and resurrection of Jesus, the Son of God.

The title, "Son of God," appears in the first chapter of every Gospel except Matthew. Mark begins his Gospel with, "The beginning of the gospel about Jesus Christ, the Son of God." In Luke, the angel Gabriel tells Mary that she will give birth to "the Son of God." Matthew tells of Satan calling Jesus "the Son of God" in his temptation of Jesus.

Mark and John not only begin their Gospels by identifying Jesus as the Son of God; they also end their Gospels with this title. In Mark the centurion at the cross declares Jesus as "the Son of God" (15:39). John closes with the reason for his Gospel: "...but these are written so that you may believe that Jesus is the Christ, the Son of God, and that by believing you may have life in his name" (20:21).

In John 1:31, the Baptist says the purpose of his baptizing is to reveal the one coming after him (the Messiah) to Israel. The Baptist sees the dove descend from heaven on Jesus. The two titles the Baptist uses reveals Jesus's *Missio Dei*. The one coming into the world from God is not an earthly ruler, king, or wise person. The one coming from the Father is the Father's sinless and only Son. He is the second Adam who, through his death as the Lamb, will bring life to all peoples. Jesus, our Savior, God's Son, accomplishes God's mission of salvation.

DISCUSSION QUESTIONS

1. How can the statements of John the Baptist help us better understand our own witness of who Jesus is?

2. How does your congregation prepare the way for people to see Jesus as the "Lamb of God" and the "Son of God?"

3. How is your life influenced by believing that Jesus is the Savior of the World?

PRAYER

Heavenly Father, we thank you for revealing your only Son who accomplishes your mission of redemption and salvation. Pour out your Holy Spirit so all believers would be bold in proclaiming Jesus as the Savior. Open the eyes of those living in darkness, that they would recognize and receive the Son of God as the Lamb who died and was raised from the dead as their Savior. In the name of Jesus, amen.

STUDY 6: The Mission of God is Accomplished through Jesus

John 3:14-21; 8:23-49; 12:32-34; 12:44-50; Gal. 4:4-7; 1 John 4:9-16; Isaiah 52 and 53

Rev. Kenneth Hennings

> *For God so loved the world, that he gave his only Son, that*
> *whoever believes in him should not perish but have eternal life.*
>
> —John 3:16

COMMENTARY

The third chapter of John begins with Nicodemus coming to Jesus at night. Jesus answers Nicodemus' greeting by saying a person has to be born from above to see the kingdom of God (John 3:3). To Nicodemus's question, "How can this be?" Jesus replies that one has to be born of water and Spirit to enter the kingdom of God. In other words, God does the work, not man (John 3:5-8). Nicodemus wants to know how this "birth from God" happens. Jesus begins answering this question with our text (John 3:14-21). It is important to note that Jesus has come down from heaven and has been with the Father (John 3:13).

There are three parts to Jesus's answer of how birth from God happens. First, the Son of Man must be "lifted up" to give eternal life (verses 14-15). Second, the Father's supreme act of love sent his only Son for the purpose of giving eternal life – not to a few but to the world (verses 16-17). And third, those who believe in

Jesus as the Savior of the world are not condemned. They live in the light, not in the darkness, and they act in truth carrying out good works in God (verses 18-21).

The *Missio Dei*, the mission of God, is clear in this text. God's mission is sending his only Son into the world to save the world so that everyone can have life in Jesus (temporal) and eternal life (in Heaven). (Two Greek verbs are used in John to declare that Jesus is sent by God – *pempein* used 26 times and *apostellein* used 18 times.) God's mission is accomplished through Jesus' death, resurrection, and ascension.

John is known for his use of dualistic vocabulary throughout his Gospel, bringing out a point by also pointing out its opposite. For example, consider his uses of "condemned/not condemned," "light/darkness," and "good/evil." This dualistic vocabulary shows us how complete and powerful the work of the Son is. There is no other Savior.

Isaiah foretold of the coming Servant who would suffer and die to heal and save. None of the Old Testament kings, prophets, nor wise people could fulfill Isaiah's prophecy. Only God could send a Savior for Israel and for the world. Jesus is the one who gives his life as a ransom for many.

The mission of God to the world is powerful. It changes the hearts and lives of people. Jesus is sent by the Father to redeem people through his death, resurrection, and ascension. Jesus is the "Sent One," the Savior of the world. This is good news! Nothing compares with the news of what God has done in Jesus for man's salvation.

DISCUSSION QUESTIONS

1. How is God leading you to live in the light and not in the darkness?

2. What activities does your congregation do in God? (See John 3:18-21)

3. Jesus is the "Sent One," and He sends us to proclaim His redemption to others. What does this look like in your life and in your congregation?

PRAYER

Missional Father, thank you for your supreme act of love in sending your Son into the world to save it. Fill us with your Spirit so that we live in your love and share that love with others, especially those who do not know Jesus. Let us be lights shining in the darkness, offering hope and life through your one and only Son, Jesus. Bless your people all over the world by making them proclaimers of your great love. We pray in the name of Jesus. Amen.

STUDY 7: Date with Destiny

2 Corinthians 5

Rev. Dr. David Benke

For we know that if the tent that is our earthly home is destroyed, we have a building from God, a house not made with hands, eternal in the heavens.

—2 Corinthians 5:1

COMMENTARY

Southern Gospel singer LaShun Pace wrote a song about his soul needing to move because of a leak in his old building. The old building, of course, is his body, and his soul needs a building that is not made by man. The first eight verses of Chapter 5 of Paul's powerful second letter to the Corinthians help us understand that God's divine gift of life is "a building from God," which is "eternal, in the heavens" (v. 1). That is who we are and that is our final destination!

Even though we "walk by faith and not by sight" (v. 7), and especially since we "must appear before the judgment seat of Christ" (v. 8), it is critical that our personal destiny is secure in advance. Our brokenness is apparent. There is indeed a serious leak in the building – we are mortal. Our most secure destination, one we know from the day we arrive on earth, is death. We are dust and ashes (see Genesis 3:19 and Psalm 103:14).

That conclusion is turned inside out by God! As Paul states, "we have concluded this: that one died for all, therefore all have died; and He (Christ) died for all, that those who live might no longer live for themselves but for Him who for their sake died and was raised."

Wait, what? you might say. *I am not waiting for death – I'm already dead and gone and back again, with and in Christ!*

Paul continues: "if anyone is in Christ he is a new creation. Behold, the old has passed away, and the new has come."

Philosophers call this an *ontological change*, a transformation of one's very being. And it is God's gift – death of self before earthly death, and life eternal in the here-and-now, as well as the there-and-then.

This is God's process of bringing us back together with Him. And who is the "us" in this date with destiny? Is it the good guys, those who somehow make it past the judgment seat of Christ on their own merits?

Well, that list is actually non-existent.

Instead, the sweep of God's mission, God's love in action, is wildly beyond our limits. It is cosmic. "In Christ," we are told, "God was reconciling the world to Himself, not counting their trespasses against them" (2 Cor 5:19) The cosmos, the world, and all who were, are, and will be in it as *homo sapiens* have been brought back to God in Christ already. For them, the price has been paid.

What remains is for everyone in our reach, the same as in every age, to be given opportunity to receive this blessed new being as a gift from God in His Son and our Savior Jesus. If your date with destiny has been secured, then you are called to God's mission as an ambassador for Christ. Because there is no greater love, no better destiny, there is no higher calling for us than to bring others to their date with destiny!

DISCUSSION QUESTIONS

1. When the Bible says the Spirit will lead you into "all truth," what's the content of the word "all?"

2. When you speak a word of witness, how do you experience and understand the Spirit's work in and through you in communication? What tools does the Spirit use?

3. Read John 3 in the context of the Holy Spirit. What is the Spirit's relationship to the cross of Christ?

PRAYER

Dear Lord, as we have been brought back from the dead to our eternal destiny of life by Christ Jesus, give us daily the strength to be about Your mission, that everyone within our reach may know the direction of their destiny. Give us mouths to speak, and wisdom to proclaim your message as ambassadors for Christ, in whose name we pray. Amen.

CHAPTER 2

ENGAGING DISCIPLES IN THE GREAT SENDING

STUDY 8: Born Again... To Bear Witness to the Light

Mark 1:1-8; Luke 3:3-6; John 1:6-28; 3:1-8; 22-36

Rev. Dr. Jerry Kieschnick

> *And the Word became flesh and dwelt among us... full of grace and truth.*
>
> —John 1:14

> *Unless one is born of water and the Spirit, he cannot enter the kingdom of God.*
>
> —John 3:5

COMMENTARY

Our home has a number of flashlights. Some work. Some don't. The ones that work shine in the darkness, enabling us to see without stumbling and falling. The ones that don't work are useless. They do nothing to help us see in the dark.

John the Baptist came to prepare the way for Jesus, to bear witness to the light, who is Jesus, the Son of God. John was the messenger of Christ, bringing light to people in darkness.

John's methodology was proclamation, in the wilderness. Sound familiar? People today live in the wilderness of sin, despair, hopelessness, worry, and wonder. We wonder: *What is life's meaning?* and, *Why are we even here to begin with?*

John proclaimed a baptism of repentance for the forgiveness of sin, always taking care to point to Jesus, the one to come after him. John was also careful to call his baptism a baptism of repentance and to emphasize that Jesus would baptize with the Holy Spirit. "All flesh shall see the salvation of God," John said (Luke 3:6).

A different John wrote the Gospel bearing his name. One of the sons of Zebedee, this John confirmed that John the Baptist came to bear witness to the light – Jesus. John's Gospel clearly says that not everyone received the light of Jesus, but "to all who did receive him, who believed in his name, he gave the right to become children of God" (John 1:12).

One of the most beautiful passages in the Bible is John 1:14: "And the Word became flesh and dwelt among us, and we have seen his glory, glory as of the only Son from the Father, full of grace and truth."

John's audiences endeavored to figure out who John the Baptist really was. The Christ? Elijah? The Prophet? John's answer: Nope. Just the one crying out in the wilderness: "Make straight the way of the Lord."

John the Baptist was sent to point to Jesus, the one God had sent. This John also clearly spoke of his unworthiness. He was unworthy to even untie the sandals of Jesus; he was unworthy to even speak of Jesus.

In the secrecy of night's darkness, the Pharisee Nicodemus asked Jesus to confirm that he had been sent by God. Jesus said: "Unless one is born again he cannot see the kingdom of God" (John 3:3).

What does this mean for you and for me? One of the reasons we were born from our mother's womb is to bear witness to the light of Christ. Our life is not just about working, eating, sleeping, and playing. It's about pointing people to Jesus, the Jesus who was sent to earth by God to be the light of the world.

DISCUSSION QUESTIONS

1. What sources of darkness surround you and the people in your life? How does the light of Christ shine in your darkness and the darkness of those you know and love?

2. What is the importance of repentance and forgiveness in your personal/family/professional life and relationships?

3. How do you as a Christian overcome any feelings of unworthiness to be a representative of Christ Jesus, Savior of the world, and Lord of the universe?

PRAYER

Dear Heavenly Father, all thanks and praise to you for being light, for sending light, for giving light. Help me be a witness to the light every day, every way, to everyone I meet, that all may see the salvation of God. In the precious Name of Jesus. Amen.

STUDY 9: Calling of the Disciples/Apostles to Christ's Mission

Matthew 4:12-22; 9:9-13; Mark 1:14-20; 2:13-17; Luke 5:1-11, 27-32; 6:12-13; John 1:35-51

Rev. Dr. Wilbert J. Sohns

> *And he said to them, "Follow me, and I will make you fishers of men."*
>
> —Matthew 4:19

> *And when day came, he called his disciples and chose from them twelve, whom he named apostles.*
>
> —Luke 6:13

COMMENTARY

The calling of the disciples by Christ at the beginning of His public mission and ministry is recorded in all four Gospels. It is a manifestation of the *Missio Dei,* the *mission of God* in the world. When He was preparing to ascend back to His heavenly home, Jesus commanded to the disciples, even as they were going, to "make disciples of all nations" (Matthew 28:19). This is exactly what Christ Himself was doing at the beginning of His public ministry: he was making disciples of Peter, James, John, Andrew, Nathanael, Philip, and Matthew.

The fact that Jesus summoned an odd crowd of fishermen and a tax collector to follow Him is both mind-boggling and insightful. As He Himself was fishing for men, He directed those

He called to also fish for men. His summons were not based on the quality of the men; He did not require that they be educated, reputable in the community, self-righteous, nor religious leaders. That's because Christ would create and shape His learners. By following Christ, these disciples were entering into a relationship with the sent Son of God. For the followers, that relationship was life-changing.

These texts on the calling of people to faith, to become learners of Christ, to come after Him and accompany Him in His mission, demonstrate that Jesus Himself takes the initiative. He brings people into relationship with Him and into a partnership in His mission (fishing for men).

The most famous line in the movie, "Field of Dreams," is the reassuring phrase, "if you build it, they will come." So often, church leaders and congregations want to operate under the same strategy. Build a traditional, new, contemporary, or pure Lutheran worship liturgy and they will come. But this mentality, as popular as it is in "Field of Dreams," fails to recognize Christ's role in initiating His mission. Christ works in people's hearts. Christ builds the understanding and application of His mission. He uses us to reach "them."

In taking the initiative, Christ demonstrated the grace of going where people are. In Christ's day, people were on the seashore. They were fishing and mending their nets. They were out on the streets collecting taxes, eating with public sinners, and spending time with people like them – people with fears and doubts. This act of grace evoked an immediate response from the first disciples: they *immediately* left their boats and nets and way of life and followed. The word "left" (past tense of "leave") comes from the same root word as "forgiveness," a type of sending or casting off. So, they *sent away* their boats and nets, etc. But they did not cast away the world.

In naming the disciples "apostles," Christ makes it clear that discipleship is apostolic. The call to discipleship is a call to the apostolate (being sent), a call to participate in the *Missio Dei*.

In his book, *Follow Me,* Martin Franzmann writes, "The apostolate does not differ essentially from that of discipleship." The call to discipleship authorizes the "followers" (or the "sent ones") to take the initiative, and just as Christ, to establish relationships. Like Christ, we are called to make disciples, to mend (repair, restore) the nets, to leave our own comfort zones and to go to where the world works, lives, plays, and eats.

DISCUSSION QUESTIONS

1. Describe how Jesus's calling of you to follow Him has been life-changing.

2. What does it mean to you that Christ has made you a partner in being "fishers of men?"

3. The disciples left their nets and boats to be co-associates with Jesus. What have you left or are contemplating leaving to partner with Jesus?

PRAYER

Missionary God, whose love sent Your Son, Jesus into the world, we praise You that Your love provided global redemption. As You discipled us through the grace of Baptism and the Word, we beg of You to keep us following and learning of Your Son. As co-heirs with Jesus, empower us ever to embrace and follow Jesus as our Savior. Help us to ever to embrace and participate in His apostolic worldwide endeavor. In the power of Jesus's name. Amen.

STUDY 10: The Disciples are Sent to the Towns and Villages

Matthew 10:1-42; Mark 6:7-12; Luke 9:1-9; 10:1-24

Rev. Dr. David Buegler

> *But go rather to the lost sheep of the house of Israel. And proclaim as you go, saying, "The kingdom of heaven is at hand."*
>
> —Matthew 10:6-7

> *And if any place will not receive you and they will not listen to you, when you leave, shake off the dust that is on your feet as a testimony against them.*
>
> —Mark 6:11

> *And they departed and went through the villages, preaching the gospel and healing everywhere.*
>
> —Luke 9:6

> *After this the Lord appointed seventy-two others... for... "the harvest is plentiful, but the workers are few... pray earnestly to the Lord of the harvest to send out laborers into his harvest."*
>
> —Luke 10:2

COMMENTARY

Have you ever wondered why we call Matthew 28:16-20 the GREAT commission? One reason to call it GREAT is because it is WONDERFUL to be *commissioned* to *mission* by our Lord Jesus Christ. Before Jesus ever stood on the Mount of Ascension and issued the GREAT COMMISSION He *sent* the twelve disciples. Then, He eventually seventy-two more, *commissioning* them into the towns and villages to preach the gospel and show miraculous acts of mercy.

The disciples Jesus sent to the towns and villages were, for the most part, uneducated, unsophisticated, weak in faith, and slow to teach their followers. But they had been touched by Jesus and they could accomplish their mission only through the authority and power of the Lord who was sending them. It was, after all, *His* mission.

When the twelve were sent out by Jesus – and later, the seventy-two – they were sent two-by-two so they could each support and encourage their partner. But more importantly, having been sent by the authority of Christ meant they always had the authority of the gospel with them, guiding their proclamation and healing acts of mercy.

The sent ones were also warned that they were going out "like sheep among wolves" (Matthew 10:16). They were warned that since this was a divine mission, there would be devil-directed opposition. And since there was such urgency to the mission ("the harvest is plentiful, but the workers are few"), the mission demanded that the disciples shake the dust off their feet when hard-hearted rejection came to them, as a testimony against those who resisted. The very action of moving on could cause those who rejected the mission to rethink and bring them to repentance.

It is important for Christ's church to see the possible extent of this sending. Luke 10:17-24 gives three wonderful encouragements for our mission. In verses 17-19 the disciples are thrilled to have seen Spirit-driven results to their work. In verse 20, Jesus tells them the greatest thrill is to rejoice in their own eternal salvation.

And then the Lord prays to the Father, rejoicing that His holy will is being done. And then turning to the disciples he said privately, "I tell you that many prophets and kings desired to see what you see and did not see it." How blessed are the sent to be in mission and to go into the towns and villages of this lost world!

DISCUSSION QUESTIONS

1. Since the sent ones were on a divine mission, they were warned about devil-directed opposition. Where do you see the truth of that warning in your personal and congregational mission work?

2. How important is it for us to recognize that the "mission of God" is not *our* mission? What false leanings do we succumb to if we believe the mission in fact belongs to us?

3. Do you think the Great Commission is called *great* because it is so wonderful, or because it is so huge? Talk about both. Why is the act of us being sent so wonderful? And why is the mission so huge?

PRAYER

Ever-living God and Father, Your heart for the lost is seen in the way You send Your church into the world. Give us confidence as we go into the towns and villages of our world. Give us the same powerful authority of Your Word and the same powerful authority of Your acts of mercy and compassion lived out through Christ-like love. Defeat the workers of darkness each day in our mission, as You did once and for all on the cross and the open tomb. And we pray for more workers. The harvest is indeed plentiful. In Your Son's holy name. Amen.

STUDY 11: Come to the Wedding

Matthew 22:1-4; Luke 14:15-24; Rev. 19:6-9

Rev. Dr. David Buegler

> *The King sent his servants to call those who were invited... they would not come.*
>
> —Matthew 22:3

> *But they all alike began to make excuses.*
>
> —Luke 14:18

> *Blessed are those who are invited to the marriage supper of the Lamb.*
>
> —Revelation 19:9

COMMENTARY

Have you noticed in the first chapter of John's gospel the use of what has become known as "come-and-see" invitational evangelism? "Come and see," Jesus says to the disciples who asked Him where He was staying (v. 39). "Come and see," Philip says when Nathanael asks him if anything good can come out of Nazareth (v. 46).

Most often the strategy for effective mission work is not God sending lightning down and dragging people into the kingdom. Rather, we see God at work in the still, small voice of invitation ("Come to me..." Matthew 11:28). We have a picture of the Lord as a Good Shepherd calling and leading His flock ("My sheep hear my voice... and they follow me," John 10:27).

However, God's gentle invitation is naturally rejected by the sinful nature of lost humanity. In the Scriptures we have accounts that speak to Christ's disciples in mission regarding those who do not RSVP. In the invitation to the Wedding Feast in Matthew 22, those who were invited first go off to their worldly pursuits. Even worse, they kill the servants who delivered the King's invitation. The servants who are left are sent out into the streets to gather anyone who would come to the feast, including one who comes with the wrong garment. This parable told during Holy Week reveals much about the heart of God and the role of missional invitation.

Luke Chapter 14 tells a similar story of a man giving a Great Banquet. One after another of the people invited turn down the invitation with excuses. The man in the parable becomes angry. He commands his servant to go out into the streets and alleys and bring in the poor, the crippled, the blind, and the lame. Even when all of these people come, there is room for more. The man wants his banquet hall full.

The account in Revelation 19 encourages the Church of Jesus Christ (His Bride) to sit at the marriage supper of the Lamb which has no end. As Christ's servants in all generations are *sent* to be in *mission*, we must remember the call, the Good Shepherd's voice, the invitation of grace given by the Holy Spirit of the living God (see Luther's explanation to the third article). And when that call, voice, and invitation are rejected, the Bride of Christ is sent into the highways and byways of this fallen world – because Jesus wants every seat at His heavenly banquet filled.

This mission has eternal consequences.

DISCUSSION QUESTIONS

1. Discuss the difference between an invitation of grace and a lightning bolt of judgement. Why does the Good Shepherd's voice call the sheep to follow rather than whipping and driving them under duress into the sheep pen?

2. Many people want to delay or deny the invitation to sit at the salvation table. What are some of the modern-day excuses they use?

3. The Bridegroom wants every seat at the heavenly banquet filled. What does it mean that the work of the Church has "eternal consequences?" Does the Church too often think only of temporal work and temporal consequences?

PRAYER

King of all kings, Lord of all lords, may Your name be praised for Your grace-filled invitation to the eternal feast. We pray that You send the power of Your Spirit into the hearts of lost souls, that wherever Your name is proclaimed, knees will bow and the invited will confess Jesus Christ as Lord. Enable Your Bride to serve the world around her in the name of Christ her Bridegroom. Amen.

STUDY 12: The Laborers in the Vineyard
Matthew 20:1-16

Rev. Dr. David Buegler

"Why do you stand here idle all day?" They said to him, "Because no one has hired us." He said to them, "You go into the vineyard too."

—Matthew 20:6-7

COMMENTARY

Toward the end of Matthew Chapter 19, Peter asks Jesus, "We have left everything and followed you. What then will we have? "(v. 27). A few verses later Jesus teaches them: "many who are first will be last, and the last first." (v. 30). Just sixteen verses into chapter 20, Jesus will repeat: "so the last will be first, and the first last."

What Jesus shares in between those verses is the parable of the Laborers in the Vineyard. Most of the details of this parable are true-to-life, but there is something unreal about the generosity of the vineyard owner. A denarius was the usual daily wage, and it was common for a vineyard owner to hire extra help when the grapes were ready for harvest. It is not difficult to understand why the workers who labored all day were indignant when a denarius was given to those who had worked only one hour.

This, however, is a mission parable about the generous grace of God. There is danger in thinking this is a parable about compensation for work given. This parable helps us better understand the mission of God. Not one of us is dealt with by our Father God according to reward based on merit. None of us gets what we deserve.

Have you ever thought about the promise given to the repentant thief on the cross who asked Jesus to remember him? The thief was given the promise of paradise in the final hours of his life, nailed to a cross.

That was a *mission moment.*

The reward for every missionary in the Church of Jesus Christ is to participate in the greatest rescue effort in the face of human history, the rescue from sin, death, and hell. There is a lot of rescue necessary before the midnight hour.

Some of us have been on the mission from the dawn of our life. Do you see people standing around at the third hour? How wonderful that the Lord helps us out by calling them. Oh, *look!* At the sixth and ninth hours, still others are standing around. Jesus asks, "Why are you standing around doing nothing?"

"No one has hired us," they answer.

So, they are sent also into the vineyard.

HALLELUJAH!

Those of us who have been working all day are not doing such an amazing job that we have the harvest field covered. God be praised for more workers, no matter when in the day they come. Those of us who are working in the vineyard need help. We need all the help we can get.

Yet, this parable is not about us. It is about the overwhelming generosity of our God in His Son, Jesus Christ. This parable is about the many people standing around, doing nothing. It is about working while it is daylight, because once the midnight hour comes, it will be a lot harder to see what we are doing.

So, the last will be first, and the first will be last (Matthew 20:16). This parable is about the mission of God.

DISCUSSION QUESTIONS

1. What is the danger of thinking this parable is about compensation for work completed? What is the danger with thinking you deserve something special if you are diligent worker in your congregation?

2. How many people are out there *unemployed* from kingdom work? Jesus asks, "Why are you standing around doing nothing?" Could it be your congregation is an "employment agency" for kingdom workers? Talk about some plans to improve the kingdom worker role in your congregation.

3. Think about your congregation as part of God's vineyard. What does it mean that your vines need to be pruned occasionally? What does it mean that your nourishment comes from the vine? What does it mean that the fruit you bear lasts into eternity? Study John 15 as you discuss these questions.

PRAYER

Precious Vine of God's vineyard, we are branches seeking to bear fruit. But we confess, unless we abide in You, we can bear no fruit. Help us to draw our nourishment from Your generous love. Prune us where it is necessary for our spiritual health. And graft unto Your holy Vine many more branches, that we all might be in mission while it is day, before the night comes. Finally, cause us to rejoice in thanks for Your overwhelming generosity of grace in Jesus Christ. The fruit that is grown in Your vineyard is *eternal*. Amen.

STUDY 13: God's Commission: Prophesied
Mark 1:1-8

Rev. Dr. Paul Maier

As it is written in Isaiah the prophet, "Behold, I send my messenger before your face, who will prepare your way, the voice of one crying in the wilderness: 'Prepare the way of the Lord, make his paths straight.'"

—Mark 1:2-3

COMMENTARY

God's Commission: Prophesied. Mark's gospel plunges directly into how God's Divine commission was fulfilled not only in Jesus Christ, but in the unique individual who was his forerunner, John the Baptizer. Clearly, the plan for introducing the Messiah via his precursor was more than seven hundred years old at the time Mark wrote, since that incredible prophet, Isaiah, seemed to be an eyewitness to so much in the life of Jesus, whom he preceded by more than seven centuries during the reign of King Hezekiah.

Theologians have long debated the nature of Old Testament prophecy, claiming that many prophesies found fulfillment in the son of a contemporary King as well as, in this case, John the Baptist. Other scholars suggest that prophecy be interpreted more directly, a manner demonstrated in the New Testament, including in Mark. Nowhere else do we know of such a desert preacher like John. Therefore, Mark's version of prophecy seems direct, rectilinear, and thus more authoritative and convincing than other explanations. (Another famous example, also from Isaiah, comes from Isaiah 9. Italics are added for emphasis: "Unto us a Child is born... and His name shall be called... Wonderful Counselor, *Mighty God, the Everlasting Father, the Prince of Peace.* If these names referred to anyone but Jesus, it would be utter blasphemy.) Clearly, in our text, Mark has Isaiah referring to John the Baptist, a direct prophecy as are most such prophecy-fulfillment couplets in the New Testament. Mark's writing is a supernatural forecast across seven hundred years, showing that the details involved in Christ's commissioning were clearly on the mind of our timeless God.

Just as God's commission centered on Jesus Christ, so it would also center especially on individuals in many of the other mission passages in the Bible. For example, consider the women in the Easter accounts, in contrast to the men, who would not believe Mary Magdalene and the women that Jesus had risen from the dead until the Risen Jesus, Himself, physically proved His Resurrection.

God's commissioning would address key individuals in the future, as well as groups involved in the various missions, especially in the most dramatic commission of all, that of St. Paul as we shall see in a future segment.

DISCUSSION QUESTIONS

1. What was Jesus' opinion of His second cousin, John the Baptizer? (See Matthew 11:11a.) Was Jesus demoting John in 11b?

2. After the Resurrection, compare the responses of the men to those of the women, as recipients of God's Commissioning.

3. What does it mean for us that we are also commissioned by God?

PRAYER

Our commissioning Lord, in communicating the faith today, we wish that we, like your Son, Jesus Christ, could have forerunners like John the Baptist, who could prepare the way for our messages about Yours, which would seem to make the task easier. And yet in Your Holy Words, we can always rely on the power of your Holy Spirit to assist us in our witness, as John did for Jesus. We thank you for assisting us yet today, sending and once again enabling us, to fulfill what you command. Amen.

STUDY 14: The Great Sending

Matthew 28:5-10; Mark 16:6-8; Luke 24:9-12; John 20:2, 17-18

Rev. Dr. Paul Maier

> *Jesus said to her, "Do not cling to me, for I have not yet ascended*
> *to the Father; but go to my brothers and say to them, 'I am*
> *ascending to my Father and your Father, to my God and your*
> *God.'" Mary Magdalene went and announced to the disciples, "I*
> *have seen the Lord" – and that he had said these things to her.*
>
> —John 20:17-18

COMMENTARY

The Resurrection accounts in Matthew, Luke, and John focus on Mary Magdalene as the "Apostle to the Apostles" at the beginning of God's Great Commissioning to spread the news of his plan of salvation through Christ, although only the destination of Galilee is mentioned. This all took place during the forty days between Jesus's Resurrection and Ascension, a fascinating period about which we know very little. At the Ascension according to Matthew, however, we have the start of the Great Commissioning of Our Creator, of which we all remain recipients today. Jesus gives the eleven disciples assembled on the Mount of Olives an absolutely limitless goal for the Gospel: that of making disciples of all nations (Matthew 28:19).

Whereas God's commissioning apparently had been limited to key individuals, it was now universalized to include the whole world. Progress toward this incredibly limitless target has advanced rapidly in the past century by the adoption of Christianity by so many people around the world. It is another stunning example of how Our Merciful Lord commands what seems impossible and yet equips His believers with the ability to fulfill His seemingly impossible commands. St. Augustine prayed: "give what you command, Oh Lord, and then Command what you will."

For the disciples, who rarely, if ever left the Holy Land, this command must have sounded like ordering a missionary today to take the Good News to the Moon. And yet the disciples were armed with the knowledge of a God who could do the impossible as demonstrated by the arrival of the Holy Spirit at the first Christian Pentecost, and the addition of St. Paul of Tarsus, who made disciples all over the Mediterranean world in one lifetime, with astounding success.

DISCUSSION QUESTIONS

1. Where have you seen the Great Commission taking place – in what nations or neighborhoods?

2. Which do you think was or is the greater challenge for Christians, the opponents of the faith in the first century or those who oppose the faith today?

3. How can we be encouraged by remembering we serve a God who can do the impossible?

PRAYER

Our Universal Lord, with cosmic gratitude we praise and thank You that You did not limit Your Commission to one chosen people, but on the Mount of the Ascension, you involve all nations, all people as candidates for salvation. St. Paul assured us that you would have all people be saved and come to the knowledge of the truth for which we, as Gentiles, are endlessly grateful even as we pray for the conversion of your own chosen people. Thank you that our own Gentile conversion was included from the very start of our Lord's ministry. Please receive our gratitude for your loving our sinful world so much that you gave Your Only Begotten Son that all who believe in Him may not perish, but have Everlasting Life, as John the Evangelist assured us (3:16). Through faith in Jesus, in whose name we pray. Amen.

CHAPTER 3

THE GREAT CHRIST SENDING

STUDY 15: Prayer Drives the Mission

John 17

Rev. Dr. Dean Nadasdy

> *I do not ask for these only, but also for those who will believe in me through their word.*
>
> —John 17:20

COMMENTARY

This prayer of Jesus, often called his high-priestly prayer, is the capstone of his upper room discourses spoken the night before his crucifixion. The movement of this visionary prayer captures the expanding mission of God. It begins with a focus on Jesus's relationship with the Father and the glory that would be His in the cross (vs. 1-5). Jesus sees His cross as a moment of being "lifted up" and glorified to draw people to Himself (John 12:32).

The mission of the church begins with "Christ crucified" (1 Corinthians 1:23). No cross, no mission.

The mission expands further as Jesus prays for his disciples (vs. 6-19). Sent by Jesus (v. 18), this little band of followers will now carry his words and acts into the world. Jesus prays that the Father will keep them in the world, lest the world perish for their lack of witness. He prays for their unity, their joy, their protection from evil, and their sacred commitment to the truth. Jesus's followers are chosen and sent for their mission in the world.

Though Jesus says, "I am not praying for the world" (v. 9), His thoughts are very much on the world in which His disciples will witness. In John's gospel, "the world" (Greek, *kosmos*) opposes God. The world does not know God (v. 25). The world cannot save itself. Left to itself, the world will perish. Its future, Jesus recognizes, is in the truth the disciples carry. You can hear it throughout the prayer: despite the world's opposition, "God so loved the world" (John 3:16).

Finally, as the mission circle expands, Jesus prays for those who will come after His first disciples (vs. 20-26). As his crucifixion approaches, the world is still on His mind and heart. He prays for the unity of His future followers "so that the world may believe that you have sent me" (v. 21). As Jesus prays, the widening circle of God's mission moves from the cross to His first followers, to His disciples in future generations, and to the world.

Gleanings from Jesus's visionary prayer for the mission of God are many. Here are just three:

1. **Unity matters in the mission.** Repeatedly Jesus prays that His disciples will be one (vs. 11, 21, 22, 23). Disunity

among disciples will present a tarnished witness to the unity of God – Father, Son, and Spirit. Conflict among disciples will take their eyes off the one who sent them. Division and competition will leave the church looking too much like the world to make a difference.

2. **Disciples must stay in the world.** You can hear it in Jesus's prayer – His concern that His disciples not escape the world (vs. 11, 15, 18). They have good reason for escapism, since the world hates them (v. 14). Disciples throughout time have considered running, hiding, and protecting themselves. Jesus is not praying for an institution here, but for a movement of courageous Christians sent into the world to witness, no matter the cost.

3. **Prayer drives the mission.** How fitting that the climax of Jesus's upper room discourses is prayer. Jesus goes to the cross speaking to His Father, certain of His Father's love. He prays "that the love with which you have loved me may be in them, and I in them" (v. 26). The mission is utterly relational and motivated by unconditional, sacrificial love (*agape*). So literally, Jesus prays on the edge of tomorrow. Prayer drives the mission.

DISCUSSION QUESTIONS

1. Where in the church today do you see disunity and competition? What pathways do you see toward reconciliation?

2. What motivates a Christian congregation to "circle the

wagons" and escape from its culture? On the other hand, what pushes a church into its mission field?

3. What can be done practically in a congregation's life to keep its mission embraced in prayer?

PRAYER

Lord, I pray for Your disciples around the world. By Your grace and calling, I count myself as one of them. Unite us, Lord, and protect us. Help us to hear You sending us each day as Your witnesses. Save us from fear and escapism. By Your Spirit at work in the Word, teach us to love the world as You love it. Teach us to pray, Lord, that in prayer we may know You more and find in Your love what we need for Your mission. In Your name. Amen.

STUDY 16: Fields Ripe for Harvest
Matthew 9:35–38

Rev. Dr. Larry Stoterau

> *And Jesus went throughout all the cities and villages, teaching in their synagogues and proclaiming the gospel of the kingdom and healing every disease and every affliction. When he saw the crowds, he had compassion for them, because they were harassed and helpless, like sheep without a shepherd. Then he said to his disciples, "The harvest is plentiful, but the laborers are few; therefore pray earnestly to the Lord of the harvest to send out laborers into his harvest."*
>
> —Matthew 9:35-38

COMMENTARY

Matthew 9 is a chapter of healing miracles of Jesus. Jesus heals a paralytic carried on a stretcher by friends. He raises from death the daughter of a ruler, and on the way to see that daughter, he cures a woman who for years had been victim to severe bleeding. He heals two blind men and restores speech to a demon-possessed man. The result of all this healing is not only restored people but great crowds who follow Jesus, some seeking healing for themselves and others who are just plain curious about this miracle worker.

As Jesus looked out over the crowds, "He had compassion for them, because they were harassed and helpless, like sheep without a shepherd" (v. 36). The *Missio Dei* is to love and care for those who are hurting, helpless, and lost. That love, direct from God, would culminate on a cross. While Jesus is preparing his disciples to take over his ministry, he teaches them by example how to love. This at times includes loving the unlovable.

Jesus points out the crowd to his disciples and uses agricultural imagery to emphasize the urgency of loving people with the love of God. Harvest time is always an exciting time. Months of hard work and prayer culminate in the farmer bringing in the fruit of his labor. Prior to the invention of big machinery, friends and neighbors would work together to harvest the crops. Time was of the essence because bad weather and bugs were current threats to the harvest. If left in the field too long, the crop might spoil.

While Orange County, California, is an urban community with 3 million people, it is still home to small acreages of land where strawberries are grown every winter and spring. When the strawberries are ripe and ready for harvest, it is not unusual to see 10 or more workers in the strawberry patch, working together to harvest the ripe fruit. Workers are critical in the field when the harvest is ready.

Knowing the urgency, Jesus says to his disciples, "pray earnestly to the Lord of the harvest to send out laborers into his harvest" (v. 38). First, he instructs them to pray. Then, he sends them out.

This text is often read at the installation of professional church workers and is certainly applicable to that setting. But this passage is not limited to the work ahead for professional church workers. Jesus points each of us to the harvest, and he calls us to work. As each of us demonstrates the love of God to one who is hurting, lonely, or lost we are participating in the harvest. We pray for workers to participate in the harvest, and we also pray for each of us to see those in our lives who need to know Jesus. Through our baptism we are called to participate in the harvest by loving people and pointing them to Christ. More important than harvesting strawberries is harvesting the people for whom Christ died as he waits to welcome them into his kingdom.

DISCUSSION QUESTIONS

1. What did Jesus mean by sending out laborers for the harvest?

2. What does the harvest look like in your neighborhood?

3. To whom is God calling you to love in the name of Jesus?

PRAYER

Dear Father in Heaven, I thank you for the gift of your Son who gave his life for me. Give me eyes to see the harvest of people who still need to know that love of Jesus, and give me the wisdom to share Jesus with them. May my words and actions help to bring in the harvest. I pray in the name of Jesus, our Lord and Savior. Amen.

STUDY 17: Finding the Lost One
Matthew 18:1-14

Rev. Dr. Larry Stoterau

> *So it is not the will of my Father who is in heaven*
> *that one of these little ones should perish.*
>
> —Matthew 18:14

COMMENTARY

Matthew 18 begins with a discussion of greatness. For the second time Jesus had told his disciples of his pending arrest, persecution, and death. Totally focused on their own needs and desires, the disciples question Jesus about who is the greatest in the kingdom of heaven. Jesus's answer of a little child identifies greatness by faith and not by human accomplishments. Jesus illustrates that faith is always in jeopardy because of our sin, which distracts us from the love of God.

Jesus turns the disciples' and our attention to those who were once in the kingdom but have wandered away or have allowed their sin to destroy their relationship with God and with the church. Bringing these people back into the fold is a critical component of the *Missio Dei*.

Jesus warns that temptation to sin and to abandon our faith is a very real part of life. When he teaches us to pray, he includes petitions to "lead us not into temptation" and, when confronted by those temptations, to pray, "deliver us from evil."

Peter reminds us, "Your adversary the devil prowls around like a roaring lion, seeking someone to devour" (I Peter 5:8).

In verses 10-14 Jesus tells the parable of the man who had one hundred sheep, one of which wanders off and gets lost. The sheep is separated from the flock by its own carelessness or foolish distraction. Sheep are followers and belonging to a flock is important for their own protection. That one would go astray would mean it was tempted toward another direction or not paying attention. It would be easy for the shepherd to rejoice that he still has 99; at least no more than one wandered off! Yet the shepherd's love for the lost sheep leads him on a fervent search. Once the lost sheep has been found, the shepherd returns with great joy, for the sheep is safe.

We live in a community of faith that is created by God in the water of baptism. In the church we rejoice as we witness another child of God being welcomed into the community at their baptism. Like the shepherd, we rejoice over one that was lost who has been found. Our heart breaks when we witness a family member, friend or member of the church being led away from the community by the temptations of the world. At times that person is led away by our lack of love and care in times of need. In verse 7 Jesus says, "Woe to the world for temptations to sin. For it is necessary that temptations come, but woe to the one by whom the temptation comes!"

The love of God brings us together. God's desire is for us to never be comfortable as one of the 99 when there is a lost sheep yet to be found. Christ not only brings us together in Holy Baptism, but he implores us to search for the one who is lost. We seek the lost sheep by loving and caring for them. And when they are found, we reunite with them with them in forgiveness.

DISCUSSION QUESTIONS

1. What does it mean for a believer to wander off from the flock?

2. Who is the lost sheep God is sending you to find?

3. How can you love this lost one back to a loving Savior?

PRAYER

Dear Father in Heaven, we rejoice in our baptism which brings us together with one another in the church. May we love one another even in times when love is difficult, and may we always seek the one who is lost, that they may return. May we never be satisfied and always searching. We seek in the name of Jesus. Amen.

STUDY 18: The Seeking God

Luke 15, Luke 19:1-10

Rev. Dr. Robert Newton

> *"What man of you, having a hundred sheep, if he has lost one of them, does not leave the ninety-nine in the open country, and go after the one that is lost, until he finds it?"*
>
> —Luke 15:4

> *And he said to him, "Son, you are always with me, and all that is mine is yours. It was fitting to celebrate and be glad, for this your brother was dead, and is alive; he was lost, and is found."*
>
> —Luke 15:31-32

> *For the Son of Man came to seek and to save the lost.*
>
> —Luke 19:10

COMMENTARY

Since Genesis 3 our God has been seeking His lost children, all of them. His question to Adam, *"Where are you?"* wasn't intended as a question about his geographic location but his relational position before his God and heavenly Father. What Adam needed to say was, "I'm lost, Father, I really am." However, his sin rendered him unable to think. Adam couldn't even think that thought, let alone voice the tragic reality.

Like Adam, our sin, too, renders us, God's children, unable to think and unable to voice where we really are in our relationship with our heavenly Father. And so our Father has and will forever seek after his lost children until He finds them.

Three times in Luke 15 our Lord Jesus impresses this truth upon His disciples and the church leaders of his day. His gracious and joyous words were set against the context of the scribes' and Pharisees' contentious grumbling: *"This man [Jesus] receives sinners and eats with them"* (Luke 15:2). They had picked that bone with Him since the earliest days of His ministry (Matthew 9). They continued to chew on it all the way to Holy Week, when *"[Jesus went] in to be the guest of a man who is a sinner"* (Luke 19:7).

That should cause us to question, in the story of the Prodigal Son, *who is the real lost boy?* (See Luke 15.) Historically, the obvious answer seems to be the son who demanded his portion of the inheritance from his father in order to leave home and squander it on reckless living and prostitutes. The story indeed reveals the lost nature of our self-centered hearts while simultaneously revealing the unconditional love of our seeking Father. *"But while he was still a long way off, his father saw him and felt compassion, and ran and embraced him and kissed him"* (Luke 15:20).

At the same time, however, we must not lose sight of the other lost son – the older brother. Consider what Jesus shares with us:

First, the prodigal son eventually came to his senses, saying, *"How many of my father's hired servants have more than enough bread, but I perish here with hunger! I will arise and go to my father, and I will say to him, 'Father, I have sinned against heaven and before you.'"*

The prodigal son was not so lost that he couldn't remember his father's kindness and generosity. He wasn't so found that he understood the unconditional nature of his father's love and incredible ability to forgive and restore. Children who are truly lost are never able to come to their senses. That's the dilemma of being lost.

But don't blame the prodigal son for his limited understanding. None of us are truly able to comprehend *"the breadth and length and height and depth [of God's grace], and to know the love of Christ that surpasses knowledge"* (Ephesians 3:18-19).

The loving father in the story never went seeking after his younger son who ran away. In reality, seeking the lost was not his responsibility; it was the older son's. Jesus tells us that the father *"divided his property between them,"* meaning that *both* sons received their inheritance on the same day. According to ancient tradition, the older brother received as much as 90% of the father's property along with the full responsibility to look after his father's extended family. He was now in charge of the estate, which included his younger brother. To better understand our Lord's intention in his third story we might paraphrase His earlier question, *"What man of you, having a younger brother who runs away, does not go after the one that is lost, until he finds him?"*

Yet, Jesus tells us, once the younger brother returned, the father went seeking after his *oldest* son:

"His father came out and entreated him," to join the family celebration.

Note that as Jesus is speaking these words, He is standing among the unhappy religious leaders, *seeking* them to come inside and join the celebration of lost sinners – their spiritual brothers and sisters – returned. In all three stories Jesus emphasized the relationship between *celebration* and *personal possession*. Listen to the father's response to the older son's complaint: "*It was fitting to celebrate and be glad, for this your brother was dead, and is alive; he was lost, and is found.*"

The father did not say, "This my son was lost," but rather, "This your brother... " Jesus wanted to impress upon his hearers the shared ownership – between Himself and us – of all those who are lost.

The real problem, perhaps, was not in the older son's inability to accept that he was his brother's keeper, but that he was his gracious *father's son.* And as his son he was the full heir of all that his father possessed, including his prodigal brother now returned. Listen to his bitter complaint: "*Look, these many years I have served you, and I never disobeyed your command, yet, you never gave me [as much as] a young goat, that I might celebrate with my friends.*" He thought of himself as a slave, not a son, as a laborer rather than a co-owner of the ranch. And though he served many years faithfully he never asked for anything, even as little as a kid goat, in order to throw a dinner party.

That shows he didn't understand his father's love, nor his place in his father's family. Why did he think his father had to give him a goat in order to throw a party? Didn't he already own the goat? Didn't he already own all of the goats? After all, he was his father's son. What belonged to his father belonged also to him. He wasted all those years slaving *for* his father out of servile obligation rather than serving *with* his father as beloved son and co-owner. Not understanding or choosing to disbelieve that he was the son of a gracious father closed his heart to celebrating his brother's return.

Our missionary motivation – as St. Paul writes in 2 Corinthians 5:14, "*For the love of Christ compels us*" – springs only from a deep and abiding understanding of our God's unconditional love for us and for all people. It does not proceed, nor can it, from some sense of obligation based on a Divine Command (Commission) or from some debt we owe God for all His graciousness to us. St. Paul sums it up this way: *"All this is from God, who through Christ reconciled us to himself and gave us the ministry of reconciliation; that is, in Christ God was reconciling the world to himself, not counting their trespasses against them, and entrusting to us the message of reconciliation"* (2 Corinthians 5:18-19).

Sola Deo Gloria!

DISCUSSION QUESTIONS

1. Reread the parable of the Prodigal Son. Picture yourself playing the role of each of the main characters: the younger brother, the older brother, the father. Write a brief description about yourself in each role.

2. At the end of the parable the father becomes the missionary to his older son: "So the father went out and pleaded with him" (Luke 15:28). Contrast the father's attitude toward his lost son(s) with the older brother's attitude toward his younger brother and toward his father. What needs to be addressed in the older brother's understanding and attitude for him to "Welcome sinners and eat with them" as Jesus did (Luke 15:2)?

3. For some time now folks have argued over the Mission of God and our participation in it. Is it by Law or Gospel? But this is the wrong question to ask. The question is not whether Christ's Mission is Law or Gospel. Christ's

Mission *is* the Gospel for the world. The real question, then, is about our participation in the *Gospel* mission: "Do we participate in His Mission by Law or Promise, by obligation or gift?" How would the older brother answer the question? How would the gracious father answer it?

PRAYER

Dearest Heavenly Father, open our hearts and minds to know who we really are and how much you really love us. From those open hearts, then, enable us to seek after our lost brothers and sisters *even as* you seek after us. In the Name of our Lord and Savior, Jesus. Amen.

STUDY 19: Christ Completes All
Luke 24:40-49

Rev. Dr. Robert Newton

Then he said to them, "These are my words that I spoke to you while I was still with you, that everything written about me in the Law of Moses and the Prophets and the Psalms must be fulfilled." Then he opened their minds to understand the Scriptures, and said to them, "Thus it is written, that the Christ should suffer and on the third day rise from the dead, and that repentance for the forgiveness of sins should be proclaimed in his name to all nations, beginning from Jerusalem. You are witnesses of these things. And behold, I am sending the promise of my Father upon you. But stay in the city until you are clothed with power from on high."

—Luke 24:44-49

COMMENTARY

For several years now a debate has taken place as to the rightful recipients of the missionary mandate, the so-called "Great Commission." Was the Great Commission intended primarily for pastors, or for all God's people, the church? Many hold to the traditional understanding that all of God's people were commissioned by our Lord in Matthew 28, Luke 24, and John 20 and, therefore, the ministry of preaching the Gospel is the right and duty of all Christians. Others argue that the Lord commissioned the eleven apostles who represent the "ordained" ministers of the Gospel; therefore, pastors rather than all

Christians are commissioned to preach the Gospel. Either way, the argument tends to ignore the most important aspect of Jesus's words: God's missionary commission belongs first and foremost to him. In line with our Lord's own testimony, the Scriptures call us to look to Jesus as God's appointed Apostle (Missionary) and Great High Priest (Hebrews 3).

Peter tells us in his Pentecost sermon that the Father made Jesus "Lord and Christ," extending His authority over all creation. Quoting King David, he proclaimed, *"The Lord said to my Lord, 'Sit at my right hand, until I make your enemies your footstool'"* (Acts 2). From this position of complete cosmic authority, our Lord Jesus continues to serve as the great Apostle, sent by His Father to complete His Father's will *that all be saved and come to the knowledge of the truth* (1 Timothy 2:4, emphasis mine). Jesus did not abdicate His commission or hand it off to someone else to complete. Sitting at the "Right hand of Father," Jesus rules over all things and continues to do so until His last enemy, death, is put under His feet and all heaven and earth, united in Him, are restored to His Father (1 Corinthians 15).

That's why it is necessary to understand that Christ's personal ministry includes not two aspects (His death and resurrection) but three (His death, resurrection, and the proclamation of repentance for the forgiveness of sins to all nations). The completion of each is guaranteed by the promise of Almighty God. Our Lord presented the sum of this promise to His disciples:

"These are my words that I spoke to you while I was still with you, that everything written about me in the Law of Moses and the prophets and the psalms must be fulfilled." Then he opened their minds to understand the Scriptures and said to them, "Thus it is written, that the Christ should suffer and on the third day

rise from the dead and that repentance to the forgiveness of sins should be proclaimed in His name to all nations beginning from Jerusalem. You are witnesses of these things."

All three elements of Jesus's mission form the *"must be fulfilled"* of God's saving work and, therefore rightly belong to the essentials of the Gospel. Thus, St. Paul confessed before King Agrippa: *"To this day I have had the help that comes from God, and so I stand here testifying both to small and great, saying nothing but what the prophets and Moses said would come to pass: that the Christ must suffer and that, by being the first to rise from the dead, he would proclaim light both to our people and to the Gentiles"* (Acts 26:22-23).

Understanding the Gospel fully requires that we include with Jesus's death and resurrection His ongoing ministry of proclaiming to the world what His death and resurrection procured.

One might ask, "Wasn't Jesus's work finished on the cross?" or, "Are we adding something more to His justifying work (the Gospel) when we state that the 'preaching of the Gospel' is an essential aspect of His ministry?"

Properly speaking, the Gospel is simply and specifically this: that through Christ's death on the cross, *"God reconciled the world to Himself, not counting [our] trespasses against [us]"* (2 Corinthians 5). Consider St. Paul's words to the Corinthians: *"For I decided to know nothing among you except Jesus Christ and him crucified"* (1 Corinthians 2:2). Christ's crucifixion is the heart and center of the Gospel. Everything we believe and confess about the Gospel, including Christ's resurrection and His preaching of forgiveness, flows out of this one fact: Christ died for all. That's why ours is called the theology of the cross.

It would be misleading, however, to suggest that Jesus's words from the cross signal that God has finished His work of saving all people. God raised His Son from the dead and declared Son right with Him. That holy absolution belongs not only to our Lord but to all who died in Him on the cross. St. Paul writes, *"For the love of Christ controls us, because we have concluded this: that one has died for all, therefore all have died; and he died for all"* (2 Corinthians 5:14). God's declaration to His Son, then, belongs also to all people, everywhere. It's essential to God that every sinner hears this Good News *personally* and in hearing it, believes and, in believing it, is saved. Indeed, Jesus' work of salvation was finished on the cross. However, our Lord will not stop working until all hear Him speak these saving words to them: "It is finished! Your debt has been paid in full!"

DISCUSSION QUESTIONS

1. Our Lord Jesus continues to this day (and until His second coming) His ministry of proclaiming God's Good News of salvation to the world. While He's the proclaimer, He uses our hearts, minds, and tongues in the process. What does it mean to you that the Lord has chosen you to be His personal voice to your friends, relatives, and neighbors?

2. By His Words, "You are witnesses of these things" (Luke 24:48), Jesus invited all of His disciples to participate with Him in His Mission. They were to "witness" to others what Jesus did (His death and resurrection) and what he was presently and actively doing in the world (proclaiming His forgiveness to all). How is our "witness" to Jesus's work the same as that of the earliest disciples? How is it different?

3. The Lord told His disciples they needed to remain in Jerusalem until they received the "promise" of the Holy Spirit, Who would equip and empower them to be His witnesses in the world. St. Peter, in His Pentecost sermon, taught that this same "promise" of the Spirit would be given to all who are baptized: "*For the promise is for you and for your children and for all who are far off, everyone whom the Lord our God calls to himself*" (Acts 2:39). What does that mean for your participation in the Mission of Christ?

PRAYER

Dearest Lord Jesus, we praise and thank you that you are the fulfillment of our Father's desire that all be saved and come to the knowledge of the Truth. As we enter your great Harvest field, help us remember that we don't enter it alone. We simply follow You, where You lead, in the sure hope that as you died and rose again, you will bring to completion all that your Father sent you to accomplish. In your Name we pray. Amen.

STUDY 20: God's Mission and Ours

John 4:1-42, John 14:12; Amos 9:13; Matthew 9:35-38;
Romans 1:16-17; 1 Corinthians 3:5-7

Rev. Kenneth Hennings

> *Many Samaritans from that town believed in him because of*
> *the woman's testimony, "He told me all that I ever did."*
>
> —John 4:39

COMMENTARY

The mission of God (*Missio Dei*) is initiated by God. No one forced God to create the world, seek Adam and Eve after the Fall, call Abraham, promise a Savior through the prophets, or send his Son as the promised Messiah. God's mission will always have a harvest, and his kingdom will always be growing (as yeast in dough). John Chapter 4 gives us a picture of Jesus initiating his saving ministry among the Samaritan people of Sychar and the sure harvest that followed.

God's mission is divided into three scenes in John 4. The first scene (vs. 4-26) is the dialogue with the Samaritan woman. (It is possible to get to Galilee without going through Samaria, but Jesus traveled through Samaria because he was on his Father's mission to be the Savior of the world.) Jesus begins and ends this dialogue with the Samaritan woman. He brings the woman from focusing on earthly water to seeing Jesus as a prophet, and then to understanding and believing that Jesus is the Messiah.

The second scene in John 4 is Jesus's dialogue with his disciples (vs. 27-38). The disciples begin the dialogue by saying, "Rabbi, eat something." Just as Jesus led the Samaritan woman from an earthly level to a spiritual level, so he leads his disciples from seeing planting and harvesting as an earthly concept to a spiritual and missional concept. Jesus's "food" is to do the will of his Father who sent him to be the Savior of the world – and the world includes the Samaritans. The mention of fields being ripe for the harvest and the reaper already gathering fruit for eternal life are pictures of the assurance of God's mission succeeding.

In John's Gospel, the harvest doesn't wait until the end of time; it is already happening in the ministry of Jesus. The same day on which the Good News has been sown, the harvest is also taking place, because the Samaritans are coming to Jesus.

The same is true today. We are called to lift up our eyes to see the harvest when we plant (sharing Jesus with others) and when we reap after someone else has planted. God has promised a harvest that should encourage all Christians to see themselves as being sent to all peoples to proclaim eternal life through Jesus, the Messiah.

Scene three (vs 39-42) is the conclusion of Jesus coming to the Samaritans to save them. The Samaritan woman shared her encounter with Jesus with the townspeople, and that led to many believing that Jesus is the Messiah. After Jesus spent two days in Sychar, more Samaritans believed because of his own word to them. "They said to the woman, 'It is no longer because of what you said that we believe, for we have heard for ourselves, and we know that this is indeed the Savior of the world'" (4:42).

Our mission is to share our faith in and experience with Jesus. We do this with ours eyes fixed on the promised harvest. Our mission work is not to get people to look to us, but to believe that Jesus is the Messiah through God's Word.

DISCUSSION QUESTIONS

1. What does the harvest field look like in your community?
2. What kind of harvest blessing is happening in your congregation?
3. How do you see yourself as being "sent" by God, locally and globally?

PRAYER

Heavenly Father, fill us with your Spirit so that we plant your Word with confidence in your promise of a harvest, whether that harvest is by us or by others. When we reap your harvest planted by others, help us see your Spirit at work among many peoples. Your mission is our mission. Empower us to plant and reap with boldness. We pray in the Name of Jesus. Amen.

STUDY 21: A Prophesy Fulfilled through Ordinary People

Luke 1:46-56; 67-79; 2:8-14; 28-32; 38

Rev. Dr. Jerry Kieschnick

> *Today in the town of David a Savior has been born to you. He is Christ the Lord!*
>
> —Luke 2:11 (NIV)

> *Lord, now you are letting your servant depart in peace... For my eyes have seen Your salvation.*
>
> —Luke 2:29-30

COMMENTARY

Isn't it amazing that in his eternal wisdom God chose to send Jesus into the world, fulfilling an Old Testament promise with (except for the Holy Spirit) the assistance of ordinary people?

Mary, the mother of Jesus, was a young teenager at the time the angel appeared to her with the announcement that she would have a child. Matthew's Gospel simply says that before she was married, she "was found to be with child from the Holy Spirit" (Matthew 1:18)

Luke describes the appearance of the angel Gabriel "to a virgin [Mary] betrothed to a man whose name was Joseph." The angel said that Mary would conceive and bear a son who would be called Jesus. When she questioned how that could be, Gabriel said: "'The Holy Spirit will come upon you, and the power of the Most High will overshadow you..."

Six months before Jesus was born, his cousin, John, was born. John was the son of Zechariah, a priest, and Elizabeth, an elderly couple who had been childless until John came along. The Bible records both Mary's Magnificat (Song of Praise) and Zechariah's Prophecy. Fascinating words that must have been Holy-Spirit inspired!

The first folks who heard of the arrival of Jesus were ordinary shepherds, watching their sheep the night Jesus was born, frightened by an angel and "a multitude of the heavenly host praising God..."

You and I would probably do the same thing the shepherds did – check it out! They went to Bethlehem, found the new baby, and told everyone they could find!

Mary and Joseph took Jesus to Jerusalem to offer a sacrifice in the temple. There an elderly man named Simeon took baby Jesus in his arms and spoke what we call the *Nunc Dimittis*.

Finally, we meet an 84-year-old widow, a prophetess named Anna, who "... worshiped with fasting and prayer night and day." She gave thanks to God for the birth of Jesus.

All of these folks had one thing in common: they were ordinary people called by God to participate in the birth of the Savior. God still uses common, ordinary people to accomplish the mission begun with the sending of Jesus. He uses you. He uses me. He sends you. He sends me. He blesses you. He blesses me.

DISCUSSION QUESTIONS

1. What do you believe that you, as an ordinary-but-God-gifted person, can do to fulfill what God has sent you to accomplish?

2. Both John's birth and Jesus's birth were miraculous events. What miracle has God performed in your life that convinces you of his love and that gives you the courage to be his representative?

3. This story focuses on the very young (Mary and two babies) and the very old (Zechariah, Elizabeth, Simeon, and Anna). What role does your age play in fulfilling God's calling in your life?

PRAYER

Dear Father, You sent Jesus from heaven to earth. His life was surrounded by ordinary people. His love saves ordinary people. Help us as ordinary people to share the extra-ordinary message of your intention and desire that all be saved, through faith in Christ our Lord, Jesus himself. Amen.

CHAPTER 4

THE GREAT SENDING ESSENTIALS

STUDY 22: Rendezvous with Jesus
Matthew 28:18-20

Rev. Dr. David Benke

> And Jesus came and said to them, "All authority in heaven
> and on earth has been given to me. Go therefore and make
> disciples of all nations, baptizing them in the name of
> the Father and of the Son and of the Holy Spirit, teaching
> them to observe all that I have commanded you. And
> behold, I am with you always, to the end of the age."

—Matthew 28:18-20

COMMENTARY

Baseball players, faced with the unenviable prospect of
professional goals which, if achieved to Hall of Fame levels,
fail to be met two-thirds of the time, invariably talk about the
process of honing their skills. For them, the results will be less

than perfect, but the journey of learning and growing in their skills continues throughout their careers. Jesus's final words to the disciples are often parsed as product and achievement, focusing on the command, "Go!", rather than on the process of being sent to make disciples.

But for the disciples in Matthew 28, Jesus's command to "Go" was all about the Divine Process of eternal destiny we know as the Mission of God. The same should be true of us today. Initiated by God, the *starting point* of mission is a rendezvous with the Crucified and Risen Lord. "Meet Me in Galilee," Christ tells the disciples, repeating for emphasis the instruction of the angel mitigated through the women to the eleven at the empty tomb (see Matthew 28:7). And there on an undisclosed mountain the sending process is unveiled for all disciples.

"Go" is not an imperative in Jesus's sending. A better translation is, *"as you go"* around the world to all nations. Jesus is effectively saying, "Eleven at the Rendezvous, as you head out on your journey, do this: *Disciple."*

As any Christian knows, the *process* of discipleship is lifelong. Teaching and learning are not structured as rote indoctrination. Why else would Jesus invite the disciples to teach others to *observe* all things He had commanded them? Observance calls for ongoing interaction, for embodying the life of Christ on a daily basis over time.

How do we know this? First, this is exactly the way the disciples themselves had been taught – on the road with Jesus, interacting, listening, watching, observing, doing what the Master did and saying what the Master said. Second, these are exactly the stories of the apostles who were sent from that mountain rendezvous to an upper room ten days later and then out into the world. Each and all of the eleven become twelve. Twelve becomes 120, and 120 becomes 3000 – within two weeks! This process of making disciples tackled the tasks baptizing, teaching, and observing from Jerusalem to Samaria to Asia Minor and all other ports of call.

How we enjoy reading those stories of God's mission in action! How we enjoy hearing of baptisms and followers moving throughout the ancient world!

Rendezvous with Jesus, then, your crucified and risen Lord. Rendezvous in your home, in your sanctuaries both virtual and in-person. And rendezvous on actual roads and on the current version, the internet highway.

Make lifelong observant followers of Christ's commands through God's grace as you follow Jesus. This is the process of the mission of God as we live out our discipling destiny.

DISCUSSION QUESTIONS

1. When, where, and how in your life did God initiate a rendezvous with you?

2. How have you been taught "on the road with Jesus" as you go about your life, and how do you share that with others?

3. Describe how you speak about God's rendezvous with you in your family setting – do you speak with your family the same way you speak with people on the road or in your community, or are there differences?

PRAYER

Lord Jesus, Ruler of our hearts, you have called us to gather and then to go forth, to undertake our life's journey following you. May we be joyful followers, speaking and acting from the urgency of your message of hope and life to all we meet on the way. Amen.

STUDY 23: Nourishing the Fishers of Men
John 21

Rev. Dr. Russell Sommerfeld

When they had finished breakfast, Jesus said to Simon Peter, "Simon, son of John, do you love me more than these?" He said to him, "Yes, Lord; you know that I love you." He said to him, "Feed my lambs." He said to him a second time, "Simon, son of John, do you love me?" He said to him, "Yes, Lord; you know that I love you." He said to him, "Tend my sheep." He said to him the third time, "Simon, son of John, do you love me?" Peter was grieved because he said to him the third time, "Do you love me?" and he said to him, "Lord, you know everything; you know that I love you." Jesus said to him, "Feed my sheep."

—John 21:15-17

COMMENTARY

Jesus said, "Feed my lambs… Tend my sheep… Feed my sheep."

The end became the beginning! John 20:30-31 seems like the conclusion of the Gospel according to John:

Now Jesus did many other signs in the presence of the disciples, which are not written in this book; but these are written so that you may believe that Jesus is the Christ, the Son of God, and that by believing you may have life in his name.

However, John immediately picks up again in Chapter 21 with, "After this Jesus revealed Himself again to the disciples by the Sea of Tiberias…"

There was more to the come. The resurrected Jesus met seven of his disciples back at their fishing vocations. He encountered them as he had done three years earlier when he had called them to be fishers of men, still failing in their vocations as fishermen. They had nothing to show for their labors. And once again, Jesus miraculously produced a fish story of all fish stories. Together, he and the disciples hauled in a net of 153 fish. John counted them!

Before they had landed this eye-popping catch on shore, Peter, upon hearing John identify Jesus standing on the shore, wrapped his outer garment around him, plunged into the water, and swam to meet Jesus. It appears John wanted to be with Jesus before his companions arrived.

Peter was surely heavily burdened with guilt over denying any association he had with Jesus. How could he ever forget Jesus's eyes looking into his own the night before Jesus's crucifixion, when he had denied Jesus (Luke 22:61)? Oh, how Peter had protested when Jesus had predicted his three-fold denial before a rooster crowed twice. Never would he do such a thing! He would rather die (Matthew 26:35)!

When Jesus breathed his last on the cross, Peter had likely thought he would be forever haunted by his dastardly deed of denial. But Jesus had overcome death. He came back. When would he confront Peter? Peter likely hoped that would happen in private. But, alas, it was not until the others had arrived on shore and Jesus had fed them breakfast that the questions began.

And the questions were potent:

"Simon, son of John, do you love me more than these?"

"Simon, son of John, do you love me?"

"Do you love me as a friend?"

Without mentioning the denials, Jesus went straight to the miserable heart of the matter. From love for his teacher to personal love and friendship, Jesus questioned Peter's integrity. It is no surprise that Peter was grieved, yes, cut to the heart!

However, we dare not miss what Jesus said after Peter answered his questions, insisting repeatedly that he loved Jesus. Jesus did not respond with, "Then prove it!" Rather, he said, "Feed my lambs... Tend my sheep... Feed my sheep."

Jesus had put an end to the guilt and shame of Peter's dishonest denials. He gave Peter a new beginning. Yes, Jesus gave Peter the privilege of feeding and tending Jesus's flock. Jesus freed Peter from the end of guilt and shame that had sprouted from the self-centeredness of sin. He freed Peter to serve his flock.

Peter would feed the little children and those new to recognizing Jesus as their Good Shepherd. He would also tend to those who were following Jesus through the nourishment of his Word. Yes, the end became the beginning for God's redeemed, forgiven and restored Peter. God gave Peter a new beginning of service.

Of course, as was his impulsive style, Peter questioned how Jesus would deal with John. After all, it was John who had made it possible for Peter to be at Jesus's trial and deny him. (John 18:15). Jesus reminded Peter to be concerned with himself, yes, with his own beginning to be Christ's witness for His flock.

Jesus has ended our guilt and shame with his own life and death. He gives us the beginning of each new day to feed others with his Word and tend them with his love.

DISCUSSION QUESTIONS

1. What specific forgiveness for specific sins have you received that fill you to overflowing for bringing the forgiveness of Jesus Christ to others?

2. What lambs and sheep are Jesus the Good Shepherd bringing into your life to be fed, tended, and nourished with his act of redemption, comforting rod and full forgiveness?

3. Who at this time in your life is in most urgent need of the gifts of Christ?

PRAYER

Lord Jesus, the true Shepherd who laid down your life for your sheep, we thank you, praise you, and rejoice in your work to end guilt and shame with forgiveness and salvation. Grant us joy in feeding and tending those whom your Spirit brings into our lives. Your end to the consequences of our sin have set us free for new beginnings each day. Enable us to direct people to you, the Shepherd who can lead them each day and into eternity. All glory to your Name, in which we pray. Amen.

STUDY 24: Holy Spirit, Divine Helper

John 14:16-27; 15:26-27; 16:5-16

Rev. Dr. David Benke

*And I will ask the Father, and he will give you
another Helper, to be with you forever.*

—John 14:16

COMMENTARY

In their song, "Holy Ghost Power," The Grace Thrillers, a
Caribbean Gospel group, sings about the Holy Ghost power
moving like a magnet. It moves here, it moves there, just like it
did on the day of Pentecost.

Frenzied movement like this is often viewed as a primary
solution for day-to-day problems of life. The Internet provides
instantaneous fixes: we can find maps, crossword puzzle clues,
recipes, home repair instructions and advice about childcare.
For those who grew up with memory verses and times tables, it
can be disconcerting to watch young fingers skip over the phone
screen and come up with answers literally in a heartbeat.

The heartbeat, of course, remains human. But the realm of
the heart remains the domain of the Lord of Life. So, when
Jesus speaks words of hope, help, and comfort to the disciples
as He enters His week of suffering, death, resurrection, and
eventual ascension, He speaks of the Divine Helper, the Holy
Spirit. The Holy Spirit will "teach you all things and bring to

your remembrance all that I have said to you" (John 14:26). The Helper does not need fact checking. The Comforter has nothing to do with fake news. In the words of our Lord, "When the Spirit of truth comes, he will guide you into all the truth" (John 16:13). That is real help, isn't it? In a world burdened with over-information and misinformation, truth matters. And the Holy Spirit brings only truth to the table. The truth he brings is everything that Jesus has said and done. Jesus's primary commandment is to love – love one another as I have loved you (John 15). Jesus' primary gift is life through the cross by which the world is drawn to Him and eternal life to those who believe (John 3).

The Holy Spirit enters human hearts by God's grace alone, as a gift. And the Holy Spirit is designed by God for us to be of help in God's mission task. What is that mission task? To communicate the power of divine love to the world.

Many feel ill-equipped to bring that message into their surroundings or find it hard in these days to deliver a Comfort-filled message when anxiety and discomfort seem to rule. But Jesus offers the divine solution for precisely that reason! The words, the witness, the message, and its power are the Holy Spirit's gift in you. John wrote, "When the Helper comes, he will bear witness about me. And you also will bear witness because you have been with me from the beginning" (John 15:26-27).

As a result, we as Christ followers have a global reach. The witnesses come from all over the world and go out into all the world, including your personal here-and-now. Indeed, the Holy Ghost power moves here and there, on your lips and mine, in witness through deed as well as word. True Help, True Hope, True Comfort!

DISCUSSION QUESTIONS

1. When the Bible says the Spirit will lead you into "all truth," what is wrapped up in the word "all?"

2. When you speak a word of witness, how do you experience and understand the Spirit's work in you and through you in communication? What tools does the Spirit use?

3. Read John 3 in the context of the Holy Spirit – what is the Spirit's relationship to the cross of Christ?

PRAYER

Holy Spirit, come into our hearts anew with the fire of Divine Love, with help for the helpless and tempest-tossed with words and care that we receive and then deliver to all within our reach. Help us, Holy Spirit, to be about the Mission of God. Amen.

STUDY 25: The Gospel Power

Romans 1:8-16

Rev. Dr. Russell Sommerfeld

For I am not ashamed of the gospel, for it is the power of God for salvation to everyone who believes, to the Jew first and also to the Greek.

—Romans 1:16

COMMENTARY

First, I thank my God through Jesus Christ for all of you, because your faith is proclaimed in all the world. For God is my witness, whom I serve with my spirit in the gospel of his Son, that without ceasing I mention you always in my prayers, asking that somehow by God's will I may now at last succeed in coming to you. For I long to see you, that I may impart to you some spiritual gift to strengthen you – that is, that we may be mutually encouraged by each other's faith, both yours and mine. I do not want you to be unaware, brothers, that I have often intended to come to you (but thus far have been prevented), in order that I may reap some harvest among you as well as among the rest of the Gentiles. I am under obligation both to Greeks and to barbarians, both to the wise and to the foolish. So I am eager to preach the gospel to you also who are in Rome.

For I am not ashamed of the gospel, for it is the power of God for salvation to everyone who believes, to the Jew first and also to the Greek.

This passage, Romans 1:8-16, demonstrates that being in debt and under obligation are familiar experiences. Paul, personally called by Jesus to serve as an Apostle, described himself as debtor, yes, under obligation. His debt was not financial and his creditor was not the holder of a loan. Paul, a Jew-become-Christian, declared his debt, yes, his obligation, to Greeks, barbarians, the wise, *and* the foolish. He was committed to paying his debt by preaching the Good News of salvation through Jesus Christ alone.

We dare not forget to whom Paul was writing. God the Holy Spirit inspired him to pen a letter to a congregation of Christians whom he had not met. Ah, he had friends from the congregation in the ancient city of Rome. His good friends and fellow tent makers, as well as missionaries, Aquila and Priscilla originated from the Roman church. Paul had a deep fraternal affection for them.

Paul also had a burning desire to visit the Roman congregation. He was fully aware of the faith in Christ the Spirit had worked among those Christians of Rome. He wanted to encourage their faith in Christ and be encouraged by their faith in Christ. But mutual encouragement was not his sole motivation for visiting these fellow Christians. Paul had harvest on his mind.

The harvest he anticipated would be among people to whom God had indebted him. Paul, a self-proclaimed Hebrew of Hebrews from the honored tribe of Benjamin, (Philippians 3:5) was obligated to those who were not Hebrews. Like today, people back then created categories artificially separating people from one another. Such categories resulted in discrimination and ridicule. To Paul, this meant he was indebted to them to pay with what God had given him; namely, the Good News of Jesus, the

Savior for all of humanity.

Preaching such Good News might seem foolish to these varying classes of citizens, non-citizens, educated, uneducated, wise, and foolish. But proclaiming the best news there is for humanity was exactly what Paul must do. It was his obligation as a Christian and one called to apostolic ministry by Jesus.

Therefore, Paul, with fearless courage, announced what has come to be known as the heart of his letter to the Christians in Rome: "For I am not ashamed of the gospel, for it is the power of God for salvation to everyone who believes, to the Jew first and also to the Greek."

Paul knew the source of the power to move every kind of person to reliance upon Christ for forgiveness, salvation, and eternal life. The power did not come through him, but through the Good News of Christ. Paul knew he was obligated to unashamedly proclaim this News for humanity.

In 1882, pastor, theologian, and seminary and church body president C. F. W. Walther preached a sermon titled, "The Holy Desire and Duty of all Christians to Lead Souls to Christ." He reminded his listeners, "Yet, my Beloved, a Christian through faith receives not only such a desire to lead souls to Christ. He also has a sacred duty... Through holy baptism a Christian has received not only power and authority and the right, but also the high and holy obligation to guard and to sustain against the loss of divine grace and to assist to the end that others are enlightened and brought to Christ, the bishop of their souls." (Walther, C. F. W.; Pohlers, Donald, trans. "The Holy Desire and Duty of All Christians to Lead Souls to Christ," The Year of Grace Sermons. St. Louis: Concordia Publishing House, 1890).

To be sure, Paul was called directly by Christ to serve as an apostolic ministry. As Walther proclaimed so long ago, so it is today: "Indeed, it is true: not everyone is a minister or bishop in the Christian congregation. God is a God of order. For the sake of order it is always required that only one or a few be chosen from the congregation and they, in the name (stead) of all, administer the rights of the spiritual priesthood publicly. However, just as in the construction of a visible church (building) the building supervisors are not the only workers who organize and lead. They necessarily have many helpers."

Like Paul, we baptized Christians are given the desire and dutiful joy of being helpers to share the hope in Christ dwelling within us.

DISCUSSION QUESTIONS

1. Why are you motivated to bring the Good News of Jesus to people of every category humans have created? Are you trying to fulfill a command? Are you living out your identity in Christ?

2. When do you find yourself ashamed of the Gospel? Why? What do you need when such shame occurs?

3. How do you continue with confidence in the power of the Gospel when you don't see immediate results from sharing it? What do you need at such times?

PRAYER

O God the Holy Spirit, work in us by the power of your Word the holy desire to be indebted to those who do not yet know Christ as their Savior for this life and eternity. Grant us the opportunities and the words we need when speaking the Name and works of Christ into the lives of people. Enable us never to be ashamed of the Good News of salvation in Christ. Instill in us confidence in the power of the Good News you use to bring people into living by faith in Jesus Christ, in whose Name we pray. Amen.

STUDY 26: Proclaimers are Sent

Romans 10; 16:25-27

Rev. Dr. Russell Sommerfeld

How then will they call on him in whom they have not believed?
And how are they to believe in him of whom they have never
heard? And how are they to hear without someone preaching?
And how are they to preach unless they are sent? As it is written,
"How beautiful are the feet of those who preach the good
news!" *But they have not all obeyed the gospel. For Isaiah says,*
"Lord, who has believed what he has heard from us?" *So faith*
comes from hearing, and hearing through the word of Christ.

—Romans 10:14-17

COMMENTARY

Chapter 10 of Paul's Letter to the Romans is a treasure chest for
the Mission of God. What's more, unpacking this treasure chest
is like finding jewel after jewel from the Lord. It is not uncommon
to become fixed on the brilliance of the shining Gospel mission
of verses 14-17. Indeed, they glow with, "So faith comes from
hearing and hearing through the word of Christ." However, we
dare not miss the strand of precious treasures of the Mission of
God shining the way to God giving faith through hearing the
word of Christ.

The treasures of Romans Chapter 10 really begin in Chapter 9
with verse 30. Paul asks and answers a question to demonstrate
how the Mission of God brings His life-transforming treasures to

people. Paul asks, "What shall we say, then?" Then, he answers: "The Gentiles (non-Jews) who did not pursue righteousness have attained it."

Some treasure hunt!

Paul points out that the Gentiles (non-Jews) get what the Jews were pursuing, without hunting for it. What do they get from God? They receive righteousness by faith. God makes them right with Him and they can rely on Him by faith in Christ, not faith in themselves. The Jews, who had God's covenant through which God chose to be their God out of undeserved love and gave them a worship pattern focused on sacrifice for forgiveness and a promised Savior, thought they had to make themselves right with God in order to attain righteousness.

However, the Mission of God is God showing people what it is to be right with Him. No one can make himself or herself righteous or perfect before God. We are always struggling, failing, falling, and dying.

Paul has set forth the greatest treasure there is: being right with God through Christ and receiving righteousness as a gift through faith. As Paul further unpacks the jewels of this treasure store in Romans 10, he makes known his heart's desire for those who think they have to make themselves right with God. He longs for them to stop treasure hunting and simply enjoy the Mission of God to rescue them through the actions of Jesus Christ.

Before Paul further uncovers the shiny gems of Romans 10, he reminds his listeners of how useless fake jewels are. Trying to obey every single Commandment and thus shine bright with self-made righteousness is impossible. It cannot be done! Paul observes this would be like going up to heaven to get a hold on Jesus and bring Him down to earth, or to go down into the grave and drag Him to the surface. The Mission of God is Jesus coming to people on earth. He came to suffer, die, and come back from the dead to ultimately overcome death.

The jewel Paul calls "the word of faith" shines with brightness in our mouths and hearts through Jesus coming to us. We depend on what Jesus did with His perfect life, sacrificial death, and victorious resurrection. We can confess, yes, affirm confidence in Him because He gives us that confidence. In addition, He helps us to rely on Him, from deep within hearts. Indeed, this jewel of the Mission of God glows within us as our hearts are set right with God. The warmth of internal peace with God made by Jesus's sacrifice is unlike any earthly contentment. It is a peace that surpasses human understanding. This fulfilling treasure of being made right with God does not stay in the heart only. It flows from the mouth with the brilliant glow of announced salvation in Christ alone.

And, even more, the Mission of God is to share this treasure with everyone. There is to be no distinction. When God inspired Paul to write to the Christians in the Roman congregation of the first century, Jews thought non-Jews had to become like them to receive the Mission of God. The emphasis was placed on what Jews and non-Jews alike had to do make themselves right with God. This is not the Mission of God. Our God is the Lord of all, giving away His treasures to all who call upon His name.

Even as Paul begins to unpack the treasures of the Mission of God with a question, he turns to four more "how" questions. These "how" questions form a dazzling chain where every link is directed to the treasure God is providing.

Link one: How can people call on God without believing God will hear?

Link two: How can people believe God will hear them if they

themselves have never heard of God?

Link three: How can they hear without someone preaching, yes, announcing God?

And finally, link four: How can the one who is to preach God's message do so without being sent?

These four links directly connect to the work of the Mission of God. The Mission of God is faith coming from hearing, and that hearing is through the Word of Christ.

This treasure is so beautiful that even the feet of those who bring it are beautiful. The Mission of God has been the same from Old Testament through New Testament. Paul draws upon the so-called evangelist of the Old Testament, Isaiah the Prophet, to remind us of how the Mission of God has always been in place to share His treasure of good news. From the moment our first human parents ran from God to be their own gods, the Mission of God was at work to give humanity His treasure in Christ.

Not all will receive this Good News of being made right with God. Many will fail to rely on Christ and His gifts, wanting instead to make themselves right and seeking "treasures" apart from God. Still, as Isaiah was in service to the Mission of God, so is Paul announcing for God:

> I have been found by those who did not seek me;
> I have shown myself to those who did not ask for me
> (Romans 10:20).

The Mission of God is to give His treasures in Christ to His beloved people, to shine His light of life, warm their hearts with comfort, and open their mouths to share His Good News with confidence.

DISCUSSION QUESTIONS

1. What do you need to be protected from in your attempts to make yourself right with God, depriving yourself of the treasures God freely offers by grace through faith in Jesus Christ?

2. What opportunities do you have with specific people right now to be used by God the Spirit to open the treasures of Jesus's life, death, and resurrection? In what specific ways can you share the treasure you have been given?

3. In what ways might God the Spirit use you in the "how" questions of Romans 10, "so faith comes through hearing, and hearing through the word of Christ? *How* then will they call on him in whom they have not believed? And *how* are they to believe in him of whom they have never heard? And *how* are they to hear without someone preaching? And *how* are they to preach unless they are sent?" (Italics mine.)

PRAYER

Dear God, our heavenly Father, thank You for offering Your treasures of making us right with You through Your Son Jesus Christ. Cause our hearts to glow with the warmth of Your forgiveness and open our mouths to declare Christ as our only Savior. Keep us in faith by hearing the Word of Christ and enable us by the work of Your Spirit to bring Your treasures in Christ into the lives of those You bring into our lives. In the blessed Name of Christ we pray. Amen.

STUDY 27:The Basis for Our Boldness
Philippians 1:12-14, 18b-30; 2:5-11

Rev. Dr. Gerhard Michael

> *It is my eager expectation and hope that I will not be at all ashamed, but that with full courage now as always Christ will be honored in my body, whether by life or by death. For to me to live is Christ, and to die is gain.*
> —Philippians 1:20-21

COMMENTARY

What is the basis for us to discover how to be bold, forthright, and confident in our witnessing?

When one looks at the record of the early church, one must be impressed with the boldness of the apostles. When Peter and John were on trial for healing a paralyzed man, they testified, "We cannot but speak of what we have seen and heard" (Acts 4:20). Upon their release, they prayed for God to "grant to your servants to continue to speak your word with all boldness" (v. 29).

The opening section of Paul's letter to the Philippians offers a basis for our boldness in witnessing to the Lordship of Jesus Christ.

In Philippians 1:12-14, we see the results of Paul's forthrightness. The whole imperial guard knows Paul is not a lawbreaker; his imprisonment is for Christ. But how can Paul not bemoan his adverse circumstances? This is far different than the plans he had for the Roman church to send him on his way to Spain, that he might do missionary work there. (Romans 15:23) Now his freedom to travel is restricted. How can Paul boldly say this has "served to advance the gospel?"

I wonder, too, if Paul did not recall the Old Testament story of Joseph, who had been sold into slavery by his jealous brothers. Years after his service, unjust imprisonment, and release, Joseph said to his brothers, "As for you, you meant evil against me, but God meant it for good, to bring it about that many people should be kept alive, as they are today." (Genesis 50:20) Paul himself had testified in a similar vein: "We know that for those who love God, all things work together for good, for those who are called according to his purpose." (Romans 8:28) Such knowledge leads him to cope with his difficulties and to witness boldly!

The ultimate basis for his boldness, though, is more than that. Paul plainly wrote, "It is my eager expectation and hope that I will not be at all ashamed, but that with full courage [boldness, or *parrhesia* in Greek] now as always Christ will be honored in my body, whether by life or by death. For me to live is Christ and to die is gain" (Philippians 1:20). Paul is confident because he truly understands who Jesus is and what He has done for him and for all people. As the Christ hymn states so clearly (2:5-11), Christ Jesus did not cling to His glory as the Son of God but submitted to what must have been the most adverse of circumstances imaginable – humble service throughout his life with an obedience ending in the most degrading of deaths, execution as a criminal on the cross. Paul knew Jesus had suffered as he did or him. He, Paul, had been ransomed from his fears and his desire to be in control with the costly price of his Lord's life.

And he knew that because of Jesus' perfect, total obedience,

God had exalted Jesus to the place of supreme authority, with absolutely everything subject to Him. He alone was the Lord. Caesar was not in control, nor were the authorities who had accused Paul. Even though Paul did not know if his trial would lead to his acquittal or execution, he was confident, because Jesus was his Lord. Paul would be neither frightened nor intimidated. He could forthrightly point to Jesus because Jesus was the basis of his boldness.

The delightful side effect was that Paul's boldness inspired many Roman Christians to boldly speak the Word of Christ without fear (1:14). The reality of having the mind of Christ (2:5) means that we are grafted into His body; we are one with Him. As a result, Paul urged the Philippian Christians to "[stand] firm in one spirit, with one mind striving side by side for the faith of the gospel, and not frightened in anything by your opponents" (1:27-28).

Our fellowship with one another in Christ strengthens our resolve to be bold.

DISCUSSION QUESTIONS

1. What adverse circumstances have you encountered?

2. How can the Lordship of Jesus Christ encourage and embolden you when you are facing:

   a. difficulties that limit your freedom?

   b. unwelcome health issues that affect not just your body but your spirit?

   c. conflict and tensions at work, in your family, and perhaps even in your congregation?

d. opposition like the Philippians?

5. How does the Lordship of Jesus Christ provide you with more than adequate content for your witnessing?

PRAYER

Dear Jesus, lead me to know and trust you as the Lord not just of my life but of all things, that with joy and confidence I may boldly testify to Your gracious Lordship to the glory of Your name. Amen.

STUDY 28: The Great Expansion of the Faith

1 Timothy 1:12-2:7

Rev. Dr. Paul Maier

> *I thank him who has given me strength, Christ Jesus our Lord,*
> *because he judged me faithful, appointing me to his service.*

—1 Timothy 1:12

COMMENTARY

Fortunately, we have an accurate record of how believers responded to God's Commissioning in the earliest history of Christianity, the Book of Acts. This Scripture is a detailed and accurate record of the Church's earliest history and concentrates on the missional journeys of the greatest follower of Jesus, Saul – later Paul of Tarsus. In his achievements for the faith as the Church's greatest missionary, theologian, and universalizer of the faith to the Gentile world of his day in the Eastern Mediterranean coast lands, Asia Minor (today's Turkey), Greece, and Italy, he was the one person in history who totally understood the general commission of God in Christ.

Paul earned his right to be an Apostle since he had fulfilled the requirements of Apostleship as one who had seen the Risen Lord and had been commissioned by Him to preach the Gospel, both happening at his spectacular conversion on the Road to Damascus. God's commissioning also targeted the least likely person in the world who would receive it; at that time no one hated nor opposed Jesus more than Saul of Tarsus. In fact, Saul had also persecuted the early Christians in Jerusalem and beyond.

Small wonder that Paul could call himself the "chief of Sinners." In his letter to Timothy, Paul shows why God did it this way. Nothing is so powerful that it can withstand God's commissioning. The second half of the Book of Acts discloses the thrilling account of how all this happened.

Timothy was Paul's own disciple, an understudy who joined him at Lystra in Asia Minor during his second mission journey. Along with Luke, Timothy accompanied Paul for the rest of his career.

Luke, our historian, shows us the statistical effects of the Divine Commission at several points in the New Testament:

- the effect of Peter's preaching in Jerusalem, where there were 3,000 converts to the faith

- to Peter and John in Jerusalem, sometime later, with 5,000 more converts

- in Thessalonica on the Second Journey, where Luke writes that Paul's Jewish opponents claim that he had turned the world upside down, for the cause of Christ

Paul would also write to the Colossians (1:3) of his gratitude to God and the joy that the Gospel was now being proclaimed throughout the Mediterranean world.

Critics have scoffed at all such statistics, especially since ancient historians have trouble *not* exaggerating statistical successes. While this is true of ancient historians generally, it is *not* true of Luke. Secular sources actually support Luke's statistics. Cornelius Tacitus, one of Rome's finest source historians, tells us in his annals (15:44) that in the year 64, when over half of Rome was destroyed in the Great Fire, that the Emperor Nero accused the Christians of starting the fire. Then, Tacitus explained who the Christians were:

> *"They were named for a Christ who was crucified by one of our Governors, Pontius Pilot, and the pernicious superstition was almost eliminated but suddenly gained new vigor and found its way even to Rome where sewage flows from all over the world."*

The point is this: The Latin term for "vast numbers" is used elsewhere by Tacitus to refer to high hundreds or thousands. This statistic is extremely important as outside testimony to the astonishing growth of the Early Church. Here in Rome, 1,500 miles away from Palestine and only 31 years after Jesus' Resurrection, a vast multitude of converts were present, and this is only the number that were arrested. It did not include the greater number of Christians who hid from or fled the horror. Such a vast population of Christians is only possible if the numbers had grown explosively as described by Luke.

In Asia Minor, only twelve years or so after the death of the Apostle John, Pliny The Younger, a Roman Governor in Asia Minor, wrote to the Emperor Trajan (AD 98-117) that there were so many Christians that the pagan temples were being deserted, "and even the country people were singing hymns to Christ as to a God."

For a faith to explode at such a rapid rate was unparalleled in the Mediterranean World and all but shouts that Luke was not exaggerating. Luke is reliable.

DISCUSSION QUESTIONS

1. In the modern world, it is widely assumed that Christianity, along with religion in general, is declining and scientific and materialistic philosophies are gaining. If this claim is true, how can we account for this rapid spread of Christianity centuries ago?

2. What evidence do we see around the world that religion in general is not in decline?

3. How might a revival be possible again in developed nations?

PRAYER

Dear Lord of History, we often refer to the "story of Christianity," "the story of the Early Church," and we have "Bible Story books" for the young. If by using the term "story" we intend only illustrations, myths or fairy tales, please forgive us. This material is *history* and not a simple, neat-and-tidy *story*. We praise and thank you for providing an abundance even of outside records, hostile to the Bible, to reinforce that your Great Commissioning is based on fact, not myth or fiction. May our response today try to parallel that of your saints of the ancient world, as we endeavor to spread the faith as they did, all with the help of your attending Holy Spirit. Amen.

CHAPTER 5

THE GREAT SENDING MULTIPLICATION OF THE GOSPEL IN ACTS

STUDY 29: God's Mission is Our Mission

Acts 1:1-11

Rev. Dr. Jon Diefenthaler

> *But you will receive power when the Holy Spirit comes on you; and you will be my witnesses in Jerusalem, and in all Judea and Samaria, and to the ends of the earth."*
>
> —Acts 1:8

COMMENTARY

According to "A Theological Statement of Mission" prepared in 1991 by the Lutheran Church—Missouri Synod's Commission on Theology and Church Relations: "Mission begins in the heart of God and expresses his great love for the world. It is the Lord's gracious initiative and ongoing activity to save a world incapable of saving itself."

This groundbreaking document goes on to assert that the chief agent whom God chose to carry out this mission to our fallen world is his Son, Jesus Christ. Through him, God entered our world "to seek and to save the lost" (Luke 19:10). Through his suffering and death on the cross, Jesus endured the wrath of God on our behalf, atoned for all our sins, and crushed the head of Satan (2 Corinthians 5:16-21). The grave from which God raised his Son delivers us from the curse of death and gives us the hope of new life, both now and in the world to come (1 Corinthians 15:55-57).

Acts 1 describes the moment that Jesus handed off this same mission to his disciples and to all of us who have subsequently become his followers. **God's mission is now our mission as the body of Christ in today's world.** The author of Acts is the same St. Luke who wrote the Gospel that bears his name, and it forms the second volume of his work. In Acts 1:1, Luke in fact tells us: "in my former book... I wrote about all that Jesus began to do and to teach until the day he was taken up to heaven." The word "began" implies that the mission of God to save our fallen world, which his Son, continues, and that Jesus is now entrusting that mission to the disciples whom he has instructed and equipped to become his apostles.

In addition, Luke tells us that Jesus substantiated this same mission "hand-off" with the "many convincing proofs that he was alive." Jesus himself had provided these proofs during the forty days following his resurrection, and by assuring them of their empowerment with the impending outpouring the Holy Spirit on the Day of Pentecost. "You will be my witnesses," he said to them. After this, Luke informs us in Acts 1:9, "he was taken up before their eyes, and a cloud hid him from their sight."

While Jesus has ascended and is seated at the right hand of the Father, he has not left the world to its own devices. You and I are the "body of Christ," the ones who carry forward what he "began to do and to teach." Jesus is in fact still with us as he promised in Matthew 28:20, present in the witness that is given to us through Word and sacrament ministries and through the witness to his life, death, and resurrection that we give to our world through what we *do* and *teach*.

Through his brief reference to it in Acts 1, St. Luke appears to link Jesus's ascension with his annunciation in the first chapter of his Gospel. At both of these moments, angels served as God's messengers. In Luke 1, the beginning of God's saving mission with the birth of his Son is announced to Mary; and Acts 1, its conclusion is foretold, as the "two men dressed in white" informed the disciple onlookers that Jesus "will come back in the same way you have seen him go into heaven."

The mission of God that our Lord has assigned to us as his church is indeed time-sensitive. Earlier in the text, Jesus admonished the disciples, who asked if the moment had come for him "to restore the kingdom of Israel." He said, "It is not for you to know the times or dates the Father has set by his own authority."

In any case, the work of carrying out the mission of God in our world is always urgent, requiring not simply churchgoers but 24/7 followers of Jesus. Speculation about the conclusion of the mission is a fool's errand. The better course for us is one described in Acts 5:42: "Day after day, in the temple courts and from house to house, [the apostles] never stopped teaching and proclaiming the good news that Jesus is the Christ."

DISCUSSION QUESTIONS

1. How does your congregation's "mission statement" compare with the theme set forth in this text?

2. In what specific ways do you see today's church partnering with God in order to further his mission?

3. What is the gospel (good news) for us that Jesus's Ascension provides?

PRAYER

O God our Father, we thank and praise you that your mission to save this world, begun through what your Son Jesus accomplished for us through his life, death, and resurrection, goes on, often despite us, and will continue until the day of his return in glory. We confess our failures as individuals and as the church to recognize that your mission is also our mission in life, and we ask that you would blanket us with your forgiveness. By means of your Holy Spirit, quicken within us and among us a renewed desire to carry your mission forward in today's broken world. Open our eyes to the opportunities you give us each day. Grant us a faith that trusts in what you promise us in your Word, a faith that relies upon the same Spirit you poured out on us at our baptisms. Help us to trust you in all that we dare to do for the sake of your mission. In the holy name of Jesus, we pray. Amen.

STUDY 30: God's Mission Partnerships

Acts 5:42-6:7

Rev. Dr. Jon Diefenthaler

Brothers and sisters, choose seven men from among you who are known to be full of the Spirit and wisdom.

—Acts 6:3 (NIV)

COMMENTARY

The text of Acts 5:42-6:7 emphasizes that the task of carrying forward God's saving mission to our world is a team effort, one that involves divine and human partnerships. The divine partner is, of course, the Holy Spirit. This is the reason Jesus urged the disciples in Acts 1 not to "leave Jerusalem," but to "wait for the gift [of the Holy Spirit] my Father promised." The rest of this same book of the Bible makes it plain that the mission of the first Christian church was Spirit-directed (for example, see Acts 8:39-40, 16:6-10, and 21:10-11). It also tells us that the apostles "never stopped teaching and proclaiming the good news that Jesus is the Christ" (Acts 5:42). The Holy Spirit had emboldened them (for example, see Acts 4:8 and 4:31). At all times, this same Spirit functioned as the "Comforter," providing the first Christians with encouragement to keep pursuing the mission to which they had been called. (See, for example, Acts 9:31.) As a result, their numbers kept increasing.

When the need arose for human partnerships to manage the

"daily distribution of food" for the growing number of widows in the first Christian community, the apostles called for the people to choose seven men from among themselves who were known to be *full of the Spirit* and wisdom. Recognizing that this was God's mission rather than their mission, they chose the seven with intention: not through a contest or a politically charged election, but with prayer and the laying on of hands.

Among those chosen was Stephen, who was later martyred for arguing at great length before the Jewish Sanhedrin that Jesus was the Messiah God had promised them in the Old Testament (see Acts 7). In Acts 8, another of the "seven," namely Philip, entered center-stage. Philip's work likewise began as one whose assignment was akin to waiting on tables. But he soon became an evangelist who, in Acts 8:6, proclaimed the Christ in Samaria.

While not explicitly stated, Luke shows us that the proclaimers of the Gospel God most desires are those who possess a servant's heart. Perhaps the greatest proclaimers of the gospel are those who know first-hand what it means to "wait on tables."

DISCUSSION QUESTIONS

1. In what ways do you or your congregation seek to team up with the Holy Spirit in your mission outreach efforts?

2. How does your congregation go about selecting its mission leaders? Compare the way your congregation selects its mission leaders to the way the apostles selected their mission leaders in the text. How do the methods differ, and which is most effective?

3. What does this text suggest about the relationship between

mission efforts that focus on people's physical needs and evangelism?

PRAYER

O God our Father, we thank you that when it comes to carrying your mission in our broken world, we are not on our own. Open our hearts, therefore, to your gift of the Holy Spirit, through whom you promise to provide us direction, strength, and encouragement we so desperately need to bear witness to the good news that Jesus brings to all our neighbors in this world. By that same Spirit, help us to identify and consecrate additional leaders "full of the Spirit and wisdom," and above all, with the servant's heart that Stephen, Philip, and their companions in Acts 6 possessed. We pray that our witness to the gospel may expand and be expressed through our actions and attention to the needs of others. In his name we pray. Amen.

STUDY 31: God's Mission is to the Whole Human Family

Acts 8:1-8

Rev. Dr. Jon Diefenthaler

> *Philip went down to a city in Samaria and*
> *proclaimed the Messiah there.*
>
> —Acts 8:5 (NIV)

COMMENTARY

There is a connection between the words of Jesus in Acts 1:8 and the *scope* of God's mission in Acts 8. While it begins with God's chosen people in Jerusalem, this mission knows no boundaries. It extends to "the ends of the earth" and includes all members of the human family. While the apostles stayed in Jerusalem, Philip became the one who ventured into the foreign and forbidden territory of the racially and religiously mixed Samaritans. Jesus had already been there in John 4, when he transformed the life of the woman at the well in Sychar. So there was all the more reason for Philip to come to an unnamed "city in Samaria."

Later in Acts 8, the Holy Spirit directed Philip to travel to Gaza in Judea, to meet with a black man from the foreign country of Ethiopia. This same man was also sexually compromised, a "eunuch" who according to the law of God in Deuteronomy 23:1 was not permitted to join "the assembly of the Lord." With the coming of Jesus as the Messiah, however, the gospel breaks down barriers of race and sexual identity, and the mission of God that has become our mission must now include all members of the human family. Here again in Acts 8:38, it was Philip who demonstrated this truth when he baptized this Ethiopian eunuch.

According to Acts 8:1, one of the major factors that prompted Philip's journey was a "great persecution" that broke out against the church in Jerusalem, one that precipitated a diaspora of many followers of Jesus "throughout Judea and Samaria." Members of the body of Christ in today's world can expect to find themselves at times on a road similar to the one Jesus took: they can expect to experience resistance, rejection, and a measure of suffering as we seek to carry God's mission forward. At the same time, however, we can in faith persevere, believing that God is fully able in some way to incorporate the adversity we are experiencing into his grand design to save our broken world. The church father Tertullian said, "The blood of the martyrs is the seed of the church." Ask any of today's leaders from the fast-growing Lutheran churches in Africa, and they are more than likely to affirm this truth on the basis of their own experience of persecution.

What just might happen, therefore, whenever we are forced to leave the familiar confines of our church-era Jerusalem and to open our eyes to the post-church world of 21st century America? If anything, Acts 8 gives us Philip's example to consider. When he "proclaimed the Christ" in Samaria with what he did as well as said in one of its cities, people's lives were changed for the better. All were liberated from the burden of their sins. Some of them were even set free from the demons that possessed them and the crippling disabilities that only could have made their daily lives incredibly miserable. As a result, Luke tells us that "there was great joy in that city."

DISCUSSION QUESTIONS

1. Where is the "Samaria" in your community? What does it look like?

2. How does the example of Philip in this text add to our understanding of mission outreach?

3. In your estimation, what is it about "persecution" that can help to further God's mission in our world?

THE PRAYER

O God our Father, we thank and praise you that your mission set forth by Jesus in his life, death, and resurrection, includes Gentiles like us as well your chosen Jewish people. Remove all of the barriers, therefore, that our sinful nature sets up in our minds and hearts, so that your gospel may have free course and be preached through all that we say and do. Help us to reach more members of the human family with your love. When resistance from others, or even the threat of persecution, to this effort arises, allow us by your Holy Spirit to trust your promise to work "all things together" for the good of your mission. In the mighty Name of Jesus we pray. Amen.

STUDY 32: God's Mission Without Walls
Acts 10:1–11:18

Rev. Keith Kohlmeier

And the voice came to him again a second time, "What God has made clean, do not call common.

—Acts 10:15

So Peter opened his mouth and said: "Truly I understand that God shows no partiality, but in every nation anyone who fears him and does what is right is acceptable to him. As for the word that he sent to Israel preaching good news of peace through Jesus Christ (He is Lord of all)... And we are witnesses.

—Acts 10:34-36, 39

COMMENTARY

This section of the book of Acts demonstrates a radical turn in the hearts of God's people engaged in the *Missio Dei*, the mission of God. In his early twentieth-century work, "The Acts of the Apostles," T. E. Page wrote, "The first grave difficulty which threatened the unity of the early Church was the question whether Gentiles desirous to become Christian need or need not first accept Judaism and the Mosaic Law."

The Spirit-directed encounter between Cornelius, the centurion of the Italian Cohort and Simon Peter literally lays the foundation for the extension of the Gospel beyond the walls of those who considered themselves the recipients of God's saving work. Peter's words reflect the commonly held belief that those not of the descendants of Abraham were common (κοινὸν) and unclean (ἀκάθαρτον).

Luke, the self-proclaimed author of Acts, is adamant about the universal nature of God's work in Christ. He demonstrates this in three ways:

1. In Chapter 2, Simeon's prayer refers to "the face of all people" (v 30)

2. The genealogy in Luke 3 is carried back to Adam; by contrast, Matthew's Gospel takes the genealogy back to Abraham (see Chapter 1)

3. the account of the Good Samaritan, which is unique to Luke

To be sure, the message is the same. Peter's "good news" to Cornelius and those whom he gathered was one consistent message. This Jesus was baptized, anointed with the Holy Spirit, went about doing good, healed those in his midst, was put to death, was raised by God, was seen eating and drinking post-resurrection, commanded us to proclaim these things, and is the one appointed to judge.

Fulfilling the commission of Matthew 28, Peter declares in v. 39, "and we are witnesses (μάρτυρες) of these things." A couple of significant points should be made here. The first is the "conversion" of St. Peter. He is turned from a man who views Gentiles as common and unclean to a man who is willing to mingle with them. The second is God's confirmation of His new work. When "the Holy Spirit fell on them" Peter would plea "Can anyone withhold water for baptizing?" (See Acts 10:41-48.)

As we take up the apostolic role in today's world we are thus encouraged, empowered, and challenged to be constantly aware of these truths. Indeed, God shows no partiality. Consider what that means in your setting and calling in your community.

DISCUSSION QUESTIONS

1. What are the "walls" that you see today that must be overcome for the gospel to have free course in our settings?

2. Can you identify personal walls that you must overcome so you can be used fully in God's *Missio Dei?*

3. Suggest one or two examples of His work that we should be celebrating outside the immediate walls of your congregation or church.

PRAYER

Missionary God, continue to open our eyes and hearts to those who are different than us. Challenge us to see all men, women, and children as people for whom Christ died and rose again. Allow our witness to herald salvation without walls, through Jesus Christ our Lord. Amen.

STUDY 33: Owning the Name "Christian"

Acts 11:19-30; Acts 13

Rev. Keith Kohlmeier

So Barnabas went to Tarsus to look for Saul, and when he had found him, he brought him to Antioch. For a whole year they met with the church and taught a great many people. And in Antioch the disciples were first called Christians.

—Acts 11:25-26

Let it be known to you therefore, brothers, that through this man forgiveness of sins is proclaimed to you, and by him everyone who believes is freed from everything from which you could not be freed by the law of Moses.

—Acts:13:38-39

COMMENTARY

There are at least three salient points in these chapters of the early church that are important to identifying those who first owned the name "Christian." The first and foundational point is based on the message these early Christians brought, which Paul lays before the crowd at Antioch (see Acts 13:16-41). Paul says: *"Let it be known to you therefore, brothers, that through this man forgiveness of sins is proclaimed to you, and by him everyone who believes is freed from everything from which you could not be freed by the law of Moses (vs. 38-39).* The central truth was the message of Jesus Christ as the fulfillment of all the promises of God, the full and complete payment for sin, and the freedom to live in response to God's grace.

The second point is that those who own the name "Christian" are a group in motion. It is important to note the passive voice of verse 19: "they were scattered" (διασπαρέντες). The verses that follow record the response of those Christians. Note how many times the words "went," "sent," "sending," "sent them off," etc. appear. Not only were these *Christians* commissioned by the church; they were "sent out by the Holy Spirit" (Αὐτοὶ μὲν οὖν ἐκπεμφθέντες ὑπὸ τοῦ ἁγίου πνεύματος) in 13:4. It was the missionary God who propelled them, and those who owned the name responded by going!

The church's core should always be in motion. From the Jews to the Gentiles. From Jerusalem to the outlying territories including Antioch. From the record of Barnabas and Saul to Saul and Barnabas.

The third and final point to clearly identifying the early Christians is that they were known for living lives of response to the saving message. According to Acts 11:21, they responded to the message by *believing* it (ὁ πιστεύσας ἐπέστρεψεν ἐπὶ τὸν κύριον). The response of the Antioch Christians was visibly evident to Barnabas. He literally "saw the grace of God" (v. 23). Paul refers to the Antioch Christians' calling by quoting Isiah 49:6: "I have made you a light for the Gentiles, that you may bring salvation to the ends of the earth" (v.47). In our next study, we will see that that response included the physical support of the Jerusalem believers. Owning the name *Christian* is not a birthright, but a commission to those of us scattered today.

DISCUSSION QUESTIONS

1. We know that "being Christian" is passive. God has acted on our behalf in Jesus. But "being a Christian" is active. Can you describe the difference?

2. Do you feel "sent" as God's child today? Why or why not?

3. What would our confirmation rite look like if we used that milestone as a sending or commissioning service for our youth?

PRAYER

Missionary God, we pray that You would continue to inspire and direct us as a people to own the name "Christian." Let our lives reflect the light of Your saving Word to our neighbors and neighborhoods in such a fashion that we too may be called "Christian." Open our hearts and eyes to those opportunities before us today, that whether through persecution or invitation, we may "continue to bring you the good news that what God promised to the fathers, this He has fulfilled." Amen.

STUDY 34: Of Councils, Conflict, Conventions, and the Mission of God

Acts 15

Rev. Keith Kohlmeier

> *But some men came down from Judea and were teaching the brothers, "Unless you are circumcised according to the custom of Moses, you cannot be saved." And after Paul and Barnabas had no small dissension and debate with them, Paul and Barnabas and some of the others were appointed to go up to Jerusalem to the apostles and the elders about this question.*

—*Acts 15:1-2*

> *Now, therefore, why are you putting God to the test by placing a yoke on the neck of the disciples that neither our fathers nor we have been able to bear? But we believe that we will be saved through the grace of the Lord Jesus, just as they will.*

—Acts 15:10-11

COMMENTARY

The saying is true and worthy of full acceptance: where two or three are gathered together on earth there will be at least five opinions. It is part of our nature, at least the *et peccator* (or sinful) nature. And its roots are clearly recorded for us in Genesis 3:1: "Now the serpent... said to the woman 'Did God actually say You shall not eat of any tree in the garden?'" And so was conflict and separation introduced into the world.

Satan continues his attack on the church, God's Word, and God's mission throughout the ages. Sometimes he leads denials of God's Word, and sometimes he attaches to it rules and rubrics that attack the saving message from within. The Jerusalem Council is but one example. The cover story is about circumcision and obeying God. But the underlying battle is about the mission of God to all people and the behavior of God's people that enables the full and free proclamation of God's saving grace.

Sadly, sometimes the very church itself restricts these truths. We all remember Martin Luther's somber response at Worms, "Unless I am convinced by the testimony of the Scriptures or by clear reason (for I do not trust either in the pope or in councils alone, since it is well known that they have often erred and contradicted themselves), I am bound by the Scriptures I have quoted and my conscience is captive to the Word of God."

It is not incidental that the Jerusalem Council appears immediately following Paul's and Barnabas's initial missionary journey into Asia Minor. The challenge of the party of the Pharisees stands as a frontal attack by the devil and his angels upon both the source and the goal of the gospel. We must not be deceived. That challenge did not end in Jerusalem or Worms. It is just as important today that we continue to pray that "Your Word may have free course and be preached to the joy and edifying of Christ's people." When Luther wrote these words of his hymn "Lord Keep us Steadfast in Your Word," he addressed the devil's assault from without *and* within the church.

Jerusalem's response to Paul and Barnabas's mission has much to teach us. First, the church listened to what God was doing through both arguments. Second, the church addressed the issue with the clear and unambiguous message of the saving Word of

God. And finally, the church encouraged the continued extension of God's grace to all. Did that end all division and discord? By no means. Note that the next verses record the division of Paul and Barnabas. Verse 39 says, "And there arose a sharp disagreement, so that they separated from each other." But also note that even then God was working to extend His saving message even more.

DISCUSSION QUESTIONS

1. The saying is true: "We need to stop deciding what to do and then asking God to bless it, and we need to start considering what God is doing and then decide to do it." What is God blessing today in the extension of His saving Word through you?

2. The zealous church leaders of Israel were known for adding laws of behavior in order to build fences around the laws of Moses. Can you think of fences that we have built that have become burdens for those who might otherwise know Jesus as their Savior?

3. Conflict is inevitable on earth, until the day of Christ's return. Think of examples of conflict in your own life. Some conflicts result in disaster and separation. Others have been the doorway to new beginnings and insight. Share a conflict from your own life or reflect to yourself on the fruits of that conflict.

THE PRAYER

Missionary God, grant to Your Church Your Holy Spirit and the wisdom that comes down from above, that Your Word may not be bound but have free course and be preached to the joy and edifying of Christ's holy people, so that in steadfast faith we may serve You and, in the confession of Your name, abide unto the end; through Jesus Christ, Your Son, our Lord, who lives and reigns with You and the Holy Spirit, one God, now and forever. Amen.

STUDY 35: Acts – The *Missio Dei* and the Beginnings of the New Testament Church

Acts 6:7; 9:31; 12:24; 16:5; 19:20; 28:31

Rev. Dr. Will Sohns

> *And the word of God continued to increase, and the number of the disciples multiplied greatly...*
>
> —Acts 6:7

COMMENTARY

After what Jesus began to do and teach (Acts 1:1), and in receiving power when the Holy Spirit came upon them (Acts 1:8), the church experienced exponential growth as recorded in six summary verses of the Book of Acts. St. Paul encouraged the brothers to pray that the message of the Lord "run" (2 Thessalonians 3:1), and Hebrews 4:12 refers to the Word as "living and active," penetrating the soul and spirit and judging the thoughts and hearts. The six summary passages in the Book of Acts are a record of how God's Word was a multiplying, progressive, and influential power of God at work in the early church. And, it is a multiplying, progressive, and influential power of God at work today.

Summary Verse 1 – Acts 6:7 (see above)

Acts 6:7 tell us that as the word of God continued to increase, the number of the disciples multiplied greatly in Jerusalem, and a great many of the priests became obedient to the faith. The *Missio Dei,* the great sending of God, is marked by the apostolic Word of the Lord, which creates and builds up the church. The power of the Word led to a tremendous increase in disciples sharing God's message of salvation. This included a great multitude of priests listening attentively and heeding the authority of the Word with complete reliance on Christ.

Summary Verse 2 – Acts 9:31

So the church throughout all Judea and Galilee and Samaria had peace and was being built up. And walking in the fear of the Lord and in the comfort of the Holy Spirit, it multiplied.

The triumphant Word of God granted peace (a prosperity) to and edified the assembly of believers (the church). The community of faith multiplied as it travelled to place after place in the fear of the Lord and in the consolation of the Holy Spirit, the promised Comforter.

Summary Verse 3 – Acts 12:24

But the word of God increased and multiplied.

As believers across time are sent into the world, it is the creative power of the Word alone that creates progress, and Christ working through us who advances the Gospel. The growth of the Word is God's plan and will.

Summary Verse 4 - Acts 16:5

So the churches were strengthened in the faith, and they increased in numbers daily.

This summary passage stresses the church once again, revealing that the newly planted congregations were made strong or were solidified in their reliance on Christ for salvation and that these assemblies of believers superabounded or exceeded in numbers every day. Again, we see that the growth of the Word is God's plan and will.

Summary Verse 5 - Acts 19:20

So the word of the Lord continued to increase and prevail mightily.

The emphasis in this passage is on the dynamic Word of the Lord, which continues to multiply in the world, proclaiming the *Missio Dei*. The Word is always exercised with force and vigor as it does its work. The growth of the Word is God's plan and will.

Summary verse 6 - Acts 28:31

... proclaiming the kingdom of God and teaching about the Lord Jesus Christ with all boldness and without hindrance.

The concluding summary passage demonstrates the ultimate goal God's great sending. The *Missio Dei* task of the church involves the believers in apostolic proclaiming and teaching freely the Lord Jesus Christ with total outspoken confidence, and with no one hindering Christ's mission to the world.

DISCUSSION QUESTIONS

1. What evidence have you observed of God's Word multiplying through your faith and life?

2. Recall and reflect on how God used you to multiply or increase the number of believers in Jesus or increased the faith of others.

3. How has your own faith grown? Describe the growth of your faith and mission.

PRAYER (paraphrasing a common liturgical prayer)

Almighty God, we ask that You would give Your Church Your Holy Spirit and the wisdom that comes down from above. We pray that Your dynamic Word, according to its nature, may not be bound, but be freely proclaimed to the joy and edifying of Christ's people everywhere in the world. We want to see Your Church multiplied so that, strengthened by You in a bold and steadfast faith, she may participate in Your mission to the world and in the confession of Your name, embrace Christ and participate unto the end. Through our sent Lord Jesus Christ. Amen.

THE GREAT SENDING NATURE AND CULTURE

STUDY 36: A Kingdom of Priests who Serve
1 Peter 2:4-12; Ex. 19:3-8; Rev. 1:5-6; 5:9-10

Rev. Gerhard Michael

But you are a chosen race, a royal priesthood, a holy nation, a people for his own possession... Once you were not a people, but now you are God's people; once you had not received mercy, but now you have received mercy. Beloved, I urge you as sojourners and exiles to abstain from the passions of the flesh, which wage war against your soul. Keep your conduct among the Gentiles honorable, so that when they speak against you as evildoers, they may see your good deeds and glorify God on the day of visitation.

—1 Peter 2:9-12

I appeal to you therefore, brothers and sisters, by the mercies of God, to present your bodies as a living sacrifice, holy and acceptable to God, which is your spiritual worship [or "reasonable service," according to the King James version]. *Do not be conformed to this world, but be transformed by the renewal of your mind, that by testing you may discern what is the will of God, what is good and acceptable and perfect.*

—Romans 12:1-2

See also Exodus 19:3-8; Isaiah 43:20b-21; Hosea 1:6-9; 2:1, 23; Revelation 1:5b-6; 5:9-10.

COMMENTARY

When God calls His people a "kingdom of priests," He highlights that they are to stand in a mediate, middle position between Him and people. As His priests, they are to represent God to the world, and the world to God. As priests, we are called to live, serve and sacrifice, to effective in our mediatorial role. Christ intervenes for us in our priesthood, helping us to pray for the world and to witness to it.

At Mount Sinai, God told the Israelites, "If you will indeed obey my voice and keep my covenant, you shall be my *treasured possession* among all people, for all the earth is mine, and you shall be to me a *kingdom of priests* and a *holy nation*" (Exodus 19:5-6, emphasis mine). Unfortunately, Israel failed again and again to fulfill this special role to which God had called them. They offered their sacrifices of bulls and goats, but their hearts and lives were often far from the Lord; they were not "doing justice, loving kindness, and walking humbly with their God" (Micah 6:8). Fortunately for us, God sent His Son into the flesh, a human being, to atone for our sins. Christ was Israel reduced to one – who, as our great high priest, offered the perfect and necessary sacrifice. His sacrifice was a life in keeping with God's will, from its beginning all the way to the cross. At the cross, He gave Himself as God's Lamb, without blemish or spot, for the world's sin. As a result, God no longer needs the sacrifice of animals.

David says, "The sacrifices of God are a broken spirit." (Psalm 51:17) In His grace and mercy, God forgives our sins for Christ's sake. He transforms us from being no one special to being *God's people*, from being without mercy," to having received mercy.

And he calls us to present our bodies as living sacrifices, holy and acceptable to God. This is our reasonable act of service (Romans 12:1-2).

Dedicating ourselves to God's purposes in the world is the fitting sacrifice God asks of us. By living in His will, we will not only do what is right; we will be exposed to the needs of the people God is sending us to serve. We will learn their joys and sorrows, their fears and failures, their struggles and successes, their ups and downs. Holding up God's love and will to their situation and needs will help us discern how to respond with wisdom and love. Being in tune with God can also very well instruct us how to carry out our other priestly roles: praying and witnessing. By knowing others' needs, we can approach God's throne of grace with our intercessions for them, and reach out to them with genuine care, rather than preconceived notions which may frustrate rather than help.

Being God's kingdom of priests means that our life on earth should be governed by our heavenly citizenship. As Peter writes, we are sojourners and exiles here. Rather than having the way of the world and our sinful nature guide our thinking and doing, let us conform our conduct to the fact that God has claimed and purchased us to be His people! Let us reject greed and slander and embrace contentment and talk that builds up. Instead of selfishness let there be generosity; rather than seeking to control, let us show compassion. Because we priests have been freed from self-centered thinking and acting by the sacrifice of our Lord, let us offer ourselves as living sacrifices to benefit and bless others.

Our place in life can be most helpful for realizing where our priestly service should be offered. Let us start at home, with husbands and wives listening and responding to each other in love.

Let parents seek to raise their children as God's children. Moving out into the neighborhood, let our relationships be marked by patience and concern, honesty, and integrity. Those same qualities can characterize our priestly service in the workplace and in society in general. There is no end of opportunities for serving and sacrificing as God's priests, seeking to represent our Lord's values and love in the world.

If the church is going to practice its identity as God's kingdom of priests, let us encourage each member to participate. We can encourage others to use the gifts and personalities God has given them, for the good of the greater Church. We are a single body. Rescued by God's mercy in Jesus Christ, let our relations within the church be marked by truthfulness and sensitivity, compassion for and commitment to one another. Just as old Israel often failed to match its conduct with its God-given identity, we too fail. We also need forgiveness to restore and grace to renew us. By such inner workings within the priesthood, we will be equipped, energized, and empowered for our life in the world.

By having our lives fashioned by God's choosing us to be His priestly kingdom, His mediators, and using our God-given gifts, we will be better able to represent God to the world. Our transformed lives will lend credibility to our witness, and the invitation to our fellowship will be warmer and more welcoming.

DISCUSSION QUESTIONS

1. How well is your worship life – both corporate and personal – helping you remember that God has called you to be His priest? Draw on the wisdom of His Word to

guide you in your thinking, speaking, and acting, so that you can represent Him faithfully in your relationships.

2. What particular challenges are you facing as you seek to represent God as one of His royal priests? What kind of support will help you fulfill your role?

3. How well is your involvement in the world alerting you to what you might address in your witness to the world and in your prayers to God for the world?

PRAYER

Dear Lord Jesus, may the compassion and mercy You have shown us sinners instruct and empower us to live as Your people in the world, serving others for Your name's sake. Amen.

STUDY 37: A Kingdom of Priests who Pray
Rev. 5:9-10; 1:5-6; Ex. 19:3-8; 1 Peter 2:4-12

Rev. Dr. Gerhard Michael

> Revelation 1:5b-6; 5:9-10; Exodus 19:3-8; Isaiah 43:20b-21;
> Hosea 1:6-9; 2:1,23; 1 Peter 2:9-12
>
> *And they sang a new song, saying, "Worthy are you to*
> *take the scroll and to open its seals, for you were slain, and*
> *by your blood you ransomed people for God... and you*
> *have made them a kingdom and priests to our God..."*
>
> —Revelation 5:9-10

COMMENTARY

Prayer is one way that priests stand as representatives between people and God. As priests, we pray, taking the world and its needs to God. Intercession is indeed a role we can play, for Jesus Christ, our great high priest, has removed our sins which would block us from getting through to God. By His perfect sacrifice, we have open access to the throne of grace. Further, through the work of the Holy Spirit, we priests are the children of God. The Almighty is our heavenly Father. We can pray confidently, for He loves us; His ears are open to our cries.

Jesus, the Son of God, shows the way. He prayed for Himself, that He might fulfill His mission: "My Father, if it be possible let this cup pass from me; nevertheless, not as I will, but as you will" (Matthew 26:39). He prayed for others as he prayed for Peter: "I have prayed for you that your faith may not fail" (Luke 22:32).

Seeing the harassed and helpless crowds, He urged His followers to pray for workers in the bountiful harvest. Surely that advice must have been accompanied by His own prayers for them.

For whom should we pray? As Jesus prayed for Himself, so should we. Let us ask God to use us as agents of His saving mission. More than likely, our service in the world will open our hearts and minds to the needs of people. Their cries for help will most likely call forth our intercessions.

Let us begin in our families. We hear the voice of the spouse who is lonely, the child who is struggling in school because she is being picked on, the aging parent whose health makes him feel useless, the adult child who has abandoned the family's faith, the family member who has lost his job – all of these and more are opportunities for our petitions.

What might we encounter in the wider society? Perhaps people who have experienced a fire or flood, who have experienced injustice because of their race, who are despondent because of the political climate in our country. The needs are many for what to pray, as are the people for whom to pray. When we think of the role of societal leaders – in government, in business, in education, in medicine – should we not include them too? Without a stable, caring society, the missionary task is much harder. With eyes and ears open, we will undoubtedly detect many in need of our prayers.

Since God's plan is to evangelize the world through His church, we dare not forget to pray for God's kingdom of priests. Let us pray for God to help them live in love and witness in Word and deed to the Lord's love for all people. And since we cannot all go to the far reaches of the world, let us include our faraway missionaries!

How wonderful that Jesus did not simply instruct us priests to pray for His mission, but that He assures that God will answer! Here is one of God's powerful promises: "Truly, truly, I say to you, whatever you ask the Father in my name, he will give it to you" (John 16:23). We can pray with confidence, to paraphrase a John Newton hymn: One can never ask too much, because we are coming to a King.

DISCUSSION QUESTIONS

1. In your network of acquaintances, who needs your intercessions?

2. How might you follow a regular routine to ensure that your role as an intercessor is not neglected?

3. The Lord's Prayer can be viewed as a "missionary prayer." As you look at this familiar prayer our Lord has given us, how might it help you pray for others?

THE PRAYER

Thank you for the gift of prayer, dear Lord! Help me use it to plead for those in my circle, that they might find in Your grace help for their challenges and opportunities for Your name's sake. Amen.

STUDY 38: A Kingdom of Priests who Witness
Isaiah 43:10,12,21; 1 Peter 2:4-10

Rev. Dr. Gerhard Michael

> *"You are my witnesses," declares the LORD...*
>
> —Isaiah 43:10a

> *"... the people I formed for myself that they might declare my praise."*
>
> —Isaiah 43:21b

> *But you are... a royal priesthood... that you may proclaim the excellencies of him who called you out of darkness into his marvelous light."*
>
> —1 Peter 2:9

COMMENTARY

What can help us witness faithfully and effectively?

If we priests are going to be effective witnesses, we will undoubtedly need to be keen observers of the people with whom we wish to share the good news of Jesus Christ. Without being with them, listening to them, and getting to know them, how will we know how best to connect with them?

And in being with them and listening to them, what might we learn about them that calls for our witness? Might they be discouraged or lonely? Perhaps they are facing health issues that pose more questions than answers. Are they struggling with a relationship? Confronting a difficult decision in the workplace?

Might they be burdened by the guilt of past mistakes? Or, might they be totally indifferent to the spiritual side of life, focused only on the here and now? What if they are quite religious but self-righteous, confident that because of their moral behavior they can face the bar of God's justice unafraid? Might they be prospering, thinking their success is the guarantee to an enjoyable future?

By listening to and cultivating a relationship with another person, we can shape our testimony to relate with her or him in ways that meaningfully connect us. We won't be people with a canned sales pitch who totally miss the hearts and minds of those with whom we are speaking. By listening carefully, we will be able, through God's grace, to share the good news of Jesus sensitively and appropriately.

The beautiful reality is that we have excellent news to tell. Peter speaks of us proclaiming the *aretas* of the "one who called us out of darkness into His marvelous light." The English Standard Version translates *aretas* as "excellencies," a word connoting noble characteristics. Other versions translate *aretas* as "mighty acts." The Greek word actually embraces both aspects – the qualities and the actions – and that is most helpful. It tells us that we have a Savior whose all-sufficient character is such that He can handle any situation any person might be facing.

Think of Jesus's qualities: compassionate, wise, powerful, meek, faithful, loving, responsive, caring, forgiving, encouraging. The list is endless. His traits are all-encompassing. Most encouraging is that those qualities get expressed in words of wisdom and hope, forgiveness, and love – and in deeds of kindness and compassion. Jesus heals the sick, restores sight to the blind and hearing to the deaf. He multiplies the loaves and fishes to feed the multitudes. He stills the storm and raises the dead. The "Light of the world" brings people out of the darkness of fear and sin into the sunlight of new life. Jesus is indeed worth sharing!

It is important for us to remember is that our witnessing is needed not only in the world, but also in the church. We believers are still this side of heaven and find ourselves on occasion slipping from saintly behavior into sinful conduct. Without the loving witness of fellow Christians to correct and encourage us, we can easily fail to promote our Lord. But with that loving witness of others, we are strengthened to proclaim the wondrous news of our Savior.

DISCUSSION QUESTIONS

1. As you relate with other people, what needs do you observe that call for your witness?

2. As you tune in to the needs of others – for instance, to guilt, anxiety, fear, or loneliness – how might you share Jesus's "excellencies," words, and actions in response to what you are hearing, sensing, and learning?

3. Read one of the Gospels and note how it reveals our Lord's character and the way He manifested it in words and actions. How can Jesus's all-sufficiency enable you to be His witness, with confidence and loving concern?

PRAYER

Open my heart, Lord, to sense the needs of others, and fill my heart with Your love that my mouth may express the fullness of Your grace to those around me for Your name's sake. Amen.

STUDY 39: Not Yet Seeing, but Believing and Rejoicing

1 Peter 1:18-25; 2:21-25; 3:18-22

Rev. Dr. Dale Meyer

> *Jesus said to him, "Have you believed because you have seen me? Blessed are those who have not seen and yet have believed.*
>
> —John 20:29

COMMENTARY

Older churchgoers grew up in "Christian" America. Going to church, knowing Bible stories, and living by the Ten Commandments were generally accepted both in and out of church. Not everyone was a true believer, but American public life had a very Christian feel to it.

"Christian" America is gone, and it's not about to come back. We can grieve what's been lost, or we can see as never before that faith is all about Jesus Christ.

The Epistle of 1 Peter contains three important passages about Jesus. The first is in Chapter 1, verses 18-25, the *Missio Dei* to you and to me. When you read these verses, notice the emphasis on redemption. It's not gold or silver, your paycheck or your retirement account, that saves you, but only the blood of the Passover victim, Jesus. The word "redeem" or "ransom" evokes the image of being freed from slavery. God's mission to you began in eternity. "He was foreknown before the foundation of the world but was made manifest in the last times for the sake of you" (1:20). These are more than sentimental, feel-good words, in the way many Americans think of faith; this is substance. Jesus, only Jesus, was sent from eternity to deliver you.

God's mission should never leave our consciousness. That's why the second Christological passage, 2:21-25, dwells more on Christ's passion, especially focusing on the injustice of his suffering and death. In doing so, Peter transitions: God's mission to us shapes our mission to others. "To this you have been called, because Christ also suffered for you, leaving you an example, so that you might follow in his steps," Peter writes. Jesus our Savior is also Jesus our Example. The Suffering Servant of Isaiah 53 invites us into his mission, even if it means suffering injustice. In America we are blessed with ways to address suffering but that's not our bottom line. Following Jesus in faith and life is, whatever happens.

Is your Lord Jesus only history? Jesus's first-century ministry is the heart of Peter's three Christological passages, but in the third passage, 3:18-25, Peter focuses on what happened after the cross, and what is still to come. As the Apostle's Creed states, "He descended into hell. The third day he rose again from the dead. He ascended into heaven and sits at the right hand of God the Father Almighty. From thence he will come to judge the living and the dead."

Followers of the living Lord are not the curators of a museum!

Peter encourages his readers: "Set your hope fully on the grace that will be brought to you at the revelation of Jesus Christ" (1:13). The best is yet to come!

"Christian" America is gone, but something eternally better is coming. "Though you have not seen him, you love him. Though you do not now see him, you believe in him and rejoice with joy that is inexpressible and filled with glory, obtaining the outcome of your faith, the salvation of your souls" (1:8-9)

DISCUSSION QUESTIONS

1. Think about the span of time that you have attended church. How has church life changed for you?

2. What are some elements of "Christian" America that once existed, but that you no longer see today?

   It's easy to forget that Jesus was an actual human being who once walked the earth. If he were walking alongside you today, or sitting at the table next to you, would you talk or behave any differently? Why or why not?

PRAYER

Lord, I love you with all my heart. I pray you will never depart from me. Encourage me continuously with your tender mercy. In Jesus name, amen.

STUDY 40: The Fear of God

1 Peter 1:13-17

Rev. Dr. Dale Meyer

And if you call on him as Father who judges impartially according to each one's deeds, conduct yourselves with fear throughout the time of your exile.

—1 Peter 1:17

COMMENTARY

This commentary is about some seldom used words. Why the Latin words *Missio Dei* instead of the "mission of God?" Because *Missio Dei* denotes a very specific understanding that captures the whole of our faith and salvation, not just a "oh, yes, there's mission too."

Here's another almost unknown Latin phrase: *incurvatus in se*. Many centuries old, it means "man (or woman) turned in on self." It's a great way to understand our sin. We habitually turn inward to our own feelings and inclinations. This is a First Commandment sin, because in turning inward we are not loving our God with all our heart. Martin Luther says, "It is easy to understand how in these things (gross sins) we seek our fulfillment and love ourselves, how we are turned in upon ourselves and become ingrown at least in our heart." But now comes the twist: In trying to live rightly before God, we believers can subtly turn in on ourselves. "We do them now not because they are pleasing to

God but because they delight us and quiet the fears of our heart, because we are praised by men, and thus we do them not for the sake of God but for ourselves" (Romans, LW, 25:245-246). "We have turned – everyone – to his own way" (Isaiah 53:6).

Second Corinthians 5:10 reminds us: "We must all appear before the judgment seat of Christ, so that each one may receive what is due for what he has done in the body, whether good or evil." Oh, that should put the fear of God into you! And that's another seldom-used phrase, the "fear of God."

The Bible uses the word "fear" broadly and often. We can understand fear across a spectrum. At one extreme is the emotion we experience when something threatening comes at us that we cannot withstand – a bad diagnosis, financial ruin, marriage on the rocks, etc. At the other extreme are similar feelings, but our attitude changes when we hear that our mighty God is coming to our rescue. God *for us*, not against us.

How do we respond to his deliverance? Wow! Awesome! And that, dear reader, is the "fear of God."

"Come, O children, listen to me; I will teach you the fear of the Lord" (Psalm 34:11).

This is good fear, wholesome fear, the fear of the Lord.

"If you call on him as Father who judges impartially according to each one's deeds, conduct yourselves with fear throughout the time of your exile, knowing that you were ransomed... with the precious blood of Christ" (1 Peter 1:17-19). The ancient term, *Missio Dei,* is most specific: Jesus turns us out of ourselves to God our Father. How awesome is the fear of God! Consider adding these seldom-used words to your faith vocabulary.

DISCUSSION QUESTIONS

1. Name some symptoms of man turned in on himself.

2. Just as we are guilty of turning in on ourselves, the church can also turn in on itself. How or where do you see this happening today?

3. How might daily "fear of God" – reverent awe that God comes to us – strengthen our mission to the world?

PRAYER

Father, you know "the thoughts of the wise... are folly." "But with you there is forgiveness, that you may be feared." "The fear of the Lord is the beginning of wisdom." For Jesus' sake! Amen. (1 Corinthians 3:19-20; Psalm 130:4; Psalm 111:10).

STUDY 41: The Honor is to You who Believe

1 Peter 2:4-8

Rev. Dr. Dale Meyer

> *So the honor is for you who believe, but for those who do not believe, "The stone that the builders rejected has become the cornerstone."*

> —1 Peter 2:7

COMMENTARY

Dr. Abjar Bahkou tells about Jason, a committed Christian who witnessed to a Middle Eastern taxi driver.

Jason's witness fell flat. The reason why is important as God wills the *Missio Dei* to come to us and go through us to others.

Jason failed at his witnessing because he used our normal way of presenting Jesus, that Jesus earned forgiveness for our sins. This is a Jesus we have come to know through regular church attendance and through reading the Bible. There is right and wrong. There is sin and punishment. But thank God! Jesus offers us forgiveness!

You are familiar with this way of presenting the Gospel because you're a product of western culture. But the taxi driver, like an increasing number of Americans, see life in terms of shame and honor, rather than in terms of sin and forgiveness.

In her book, *Dare to Lead*, Brené Brown writes, "The majority of shame researchers and clinicians agree that the difference between shame and guilt is best understood as the difference between 'I am bad' and 'I did something bad.' Guilt = I did something bad. Shame = I am bad" (128).

First Peter was written to people who knew shame. Many recipients of the epistle were Jewish Christians. Romans lumped Christians into their snobbery about Jews, judging them a superstitious people with strange customs. When many Jews and Christians refused to participate in some civic functions and revelries (such as sacrifices to the emperor and wild partying), the Romans were suspicious that these strange people were undermining society's common good. Some Christians were lowly slaves (2:18). Some were believing wives who flaunted their husbands' authority by becoming Christian, which raised eyebrows (3:1-6). And few of these dishonored believers had rights, because they weren't Roman citizens. They knew shame!

Shame was an inroad for Peter to encourage these Christians, because their Lord Jesus himself experienced shame. "As you come to him, a living stone rejected by men but in the sight of God chosen and precious, you yourselves like living stones are being built up as a spiritual house, to be a holy priesthood, to offer spiritual sacrifices acceptable to God through Jesus Christ," Peter wrote. "For it stands in Scripture: 'Behold, I am laying in Zion a stone, a cornerstone chosen and precious, and whoever believes in him will not be put to shame.' So the honor is for you who believe" (2:4-7).

Do we minimize forgiveness in witness to people from different cultures? No. Shame and honor easily relate to the forgiveness of sin, which indeed is the heart of biblical faith. When you honor God, you'll seek to obey Him. When you dishonor God, you'll disobey His commandments. You'll sin and you'll need forgiveness. How rich the fullness of the Gospel!

Jason discovered that. Awareness of shame and honor can enhance our faith and witness to Jesus.

DISCUSSION QUESTIONS

1. Has your life as a Christian been spent within the cocoon of one culture? Explain.

2. Forgiveness is foundational, but it doesn't always communicate to others. How should this encourage us to go deeper in Bible study?

3. List biblical examples of Jesus giving honor instead of shame.

PRAYER

Spirit of God, rest upon us so that our faith, "more precious than gold which perishes, may be found to result in praise and glory and honor at the revelation of Jesus Christ." Amen. (1 Peter 1:7).

STUDY 42: A Panoramic View of God's Love for the World

Rev. 5:9; 7:9; 10:11; 11:9; 13:7; 14:6; 17:15

Rev. Dr. Will Sohns

> After this I looked, and behold, a great multitude that no one could number, from every nation, from all tribes and peoples and languages, standing before the throne and before the Lamb, clothed in white robes, with palm branches in their hands...
>
> —Revelation 7:9

> Then I saw another angel flying directly overhead, with an eternal gospel to proclaim to those who dwell on earth, to every nation and tribe and language and people.
>
> —Revelation 14:6

COMMENTARY

One of the joys our family had in living in the Rocky Mountains for years was to park along the mountain highways at special turnouts to take in the panoramic views. The unobstructed views of the valleys, meadows, and steams below, the snow-capped mountains, the pine and aspen trees, were breathtaking. The view was worth every second we took to let the beauty and the vastness press in on us.

In the Book of Revelation, St. John provided the breathtaking view of the *world*, which God so dearly loves. Indeed, John powerfully illustrated that love in Chapter 3 of his Gospel: *For*

God so loved the world, that he gave his only Son... that the world might be saved through him (vs. 16-17). We see that all-encompassing love at work with the panoramic view in Revelation 5:9, with *every tribe and language and people and nation.* And we see it in Revelation 7:9: *a great multitude that no one could number, from every nation, from all tribes and peoples and languages, standing before the throne and before the Lamb.*

What a *Missio Dei* panorama! Jesus shed His blood and purchased everyone of common descent, common language, common history. He won people from every constitution, and every common custom and social mores. John's panoramic vision was of a multitude wearing robes that had been made white by the blood of the Lamb, with palms in their hands signifying eternal life... *and crying out with a loud voice, "Salvation belongs to our God who sits on the throne, and to the Lamb"* (Revelation 7:10)!

The Revelation passages reflect God's mission worldview in Christ. His heart's desire is that every people be saved: *Greeks and non-Greeks, wise and foolish* (Romans 1:14), *slave, free, male, female* (Galatians 3:28), *circumcised, uncircumcised, or barbarian* (Colossians 3:11). God wants the world, with no distinctions, partiality, or limitations. The sent Lamb of God ransomed everyone.

God's revealed mission view of heaven is spectacular. His loving heaven view is His worldview and His heart's desire is for every people to be saved. His world view of "saved" is His heaven view to never again hunger nor thirst, nor suffer scorching sun and heat but to be led by the eternal Shepherd to springs of living water with every tear wiped from the eyes (Revelation 7:16-17). God holds this panoramic heaven view for everyone.

The panoramic view of God's love for the world is breathtaking from yet another observation turnout-view. Christ conquers the great dragon, Satan, the deceiver and imitator of God. He destroys Satan's world powers and evil forces, which are determined to *destroy* every tribe and people and language and nation (Revelation 13:7) and to *prostitute* the peoples and multitudes and nations and languages (Revelation 17:15).

Another unobstructed view Christ holds is of the believers below, who live in the valley of the world. We see another angel flying directly overhead, with an eternal gospel to proclaim to those who dwell on earth, to every nation and tribe and language and people (see Revelation 10:11). Every believer (not just Luther or the clergy) who has been saved possesses the eternal Gospel. The panoramic view is clear: the *Missio Dei* involves every believer and assembly of believers in the great sending task of proclaiming the Gospel of Christ to those who dwell on earth, to every nation and tribe and language and people.

DISCUSSION QUESTIONS

1. How would you describe the view the world has of God, Christianity, and "heaven?"

2. Think about the panoramic view God has of you. How does that differ from His view of the world?

3. Describe your own panoramic view of your participation in Christ's mission.

PRAYER

Dear Christ, the Sent One, may Your angel, the Church, continue to possess the eternal Gospel and aggressively participate in Your mission to proclaim You, the divine apostle (ἀπόστολος), to those who dwell on earth, to every nation and tribe and language and people. In Your apostolic authority we pray. Amen.

CHAPTER 7

NAILING TWELVE MISSION THESES TO THE CHURCH DOOR

INTRODUCTION

Nailing Twelve Theses to the Church Door is based on and reflects work initially authored by Drs. Dean Nadasdy and Robert Newton on behalf of past gatherings of missional leaders. These theses were largely formed from two theological works – "... Prayerful Vision for the Future... LCMS" (Dean Nadasdy lead author) and "A Theological Statement" (Robert Newton lead author), as well as ad hoc conversations during missional conferences between 2017 and 2019. (Both resources are available on the website www.thegreatsending.org.) To fully appreciate the twelve theses, the reader must understand the following:

1. The theses provide a succinct definition of the *Missio Dei* based on the Word

2. The theses provide an identity of who we are as a *Missio Dei*, missional, apostolic people

3. The theses provide a declaration, making known publicly

the confessed nature of the one holy Christian *apostolic* church to fellow Christians and "institutional" Christian churches, including The Lutheran Church—Missouri Synod but also to the church-at-large

4. The theses provide a missional statement in the context of past and current *Missio Dei* misconceptions, faulty mindsets, and behaviors

5. The 42 *Missio Dei* Biblical Immersion Studies provide a basis for and the Scriptural back-up of the theses

6. The theses provide an opportunity and invite subscription by others during or after the immersion – a multitude of missional leaders together *nailing it*

7. The theses provide an opportunity to affirm "Here we stand" for the sake of Christ's mission and assert *Soli Deo Gloria*

Bible references for each of the twelve theses are listed at the end of this section.

THE TWELVE MISSION THESES

1. We believe, teach, and confess that God's mission (the *Missio Dei*, which belongs to Him and His love for the world) centers in the person and work of our Lord Jesus Christ (John 3:16-17).

2. We believe, teach, and confess that God's love has given His apostolic authority to Christ to carry out the mission to administer forgiveness of sins and eternal life to the whole world (John 17:1-3; Luke 4:18-19; 24:45-49;

Matthew 28:18-20). The truth, *freely justified for Christ's sake through faith* (see the *Augsburg Confession IV* – Justification (Tappert)), is Christianity's central teaching. All other doctrines are antecedent or consequent.

3. We believe, teach, and confess that all who are baptized in Christ are co-heirs and co-associates with Christ and participate in God's mission in relation to and through Him alone (1 Corinthians 1:9; 3:1-23).

4. We believe, teach, and confess that the *Missio Dei* is the primary lens through which we read the Scriptures, and which determines our mission being, purpose, and witness, individually and collectively (self-governing congregations) as a fellowship of the baptized in Christ (John 17:1-3, 17-20).

5. We believe, teach, and confess that just as God the Father *sent* (*apostello*) His Son Jesus into the world, Jesus *sends* all believers into the world to "seek and save the lost" (John 20:21-23; Luke 19:10).

6. We believe, teach, and confess that the Lord tells us by word and example that the Gospel must be *sent* to the unsaved if they are to hear and be saved (Romans 1:16; 10:14-17) and that the unsaved will not on their own find their way to church in order to hear the Gospel.

7. We believe, teach, and confess that the divine *sending* includes the *sending* of the Holy Spirit to empower the *sent* into their everyday world and lives to "proclaim the excellencies of him who called [them] out of darkness into his marvelous light" (1 Peter 2:9).

8. We believe, teach, and confess that the Lord continues to call His church from the nations (*Una Sancta*) around the world to work mutually in *sending* and receiving "laborers for the harvest" until that day when our Lord's mission is complete (Ephesians 4:1-7; Matthew 9:35-10:1).

9. We believe, teach, and confess that all matters of ritual, programs, and practice(s) are not the essential core of God's mission, nor is the core of God's mission mere performance(s) or the presence of liturgical, ministry or missional exercises and activities (Luke 24:45-47; Ephesians 2:8-9; 1 Corinthians 1:18-31).

10. We believe, teach, and confess that the focus of the church's sending mission and ministry(ies) is on God's love and mission (*sending*) to the whole world through Christ and not on institutional maintenance, survival, doctrinal purity, or self-interest (Matthew 16:17-19; John 15:12-13; 2 Corinthians 5:18-20; 1 John 4).

11. We believe, teach, and confess that the mission of the church is driven and empowered by the Gospel of Christ alone and Scripture, God's strong Word alone, as the sole authority for our mission, teaching, witness, and confession (refer to the *Confessions of the Evangelical Lutheran Church*) and not by legalism, individualism, separatism, and clericalism, nor by any human authority, power, control, persuasion, or any hierarchy (Romans 1:16; John 5:39; 17:17-19; Galatians 5:1).

12. We believe, teach, and confess that God gives His church a wide variety of gifts and people for the *Missio Dei*, with unique contributions of people of all ethnic backgrounds

in the culture of our life together (1 Corinthians 12; Romans 12).

BIBLE REFERENCES FOR THE TWELVE MISSION THESES

1. **John 3:16-17** "For God so loved the world, that he gave his only Son, that whoever believes in him should not perish but have eternal life. For God did not send his Son into the world to condemn the world, but in order that the world might be saved through him."

2. **John 17:1-3** "When Jesus had spoken these words, he lifted up his eyes to heaven, and said, 'Father, the hour has come; glorify your Son that the Son may glorify you, since you have given him authority over all flesh, to give eternal life to all whom you have given him. And this is eternal life, that they know you the only true God, and Jesus Christ whom you have sent.'"
Luke 4:18-19 "The Spirit of the Lord is upon me, because he has anointed me to proclaim good news to the poor. He has sent me to proclaim liberty to the captives and recovering of sight to the blind, to set at liberty those who are oppressed, to proclaim the year of the Lord's favor."
Luke 24:45-49 "Then he opened their minds to understand the Scriptures, and said to them, 'Thus it is written, that the Christ should suffer and on the third day rise from the dead, and that repentance and forgiveness of sins should be proclaimed in his name to all nations, beginning from Jerusalem. You are witnesses of these things. And behold, I am sending the promise of my Father upon you. But stay in the city until you are clothed with power from on high.'"

Matthew 28:18-20 "And Jesus came and said to them, 'All authority in heaven and on earth has been given to me. Go therefore and make disciples of all nations, baptizing them in the name of the Father and of the Son and of the Holy Spirit, teaching them to observe all that I have commanded you. And behold, I am with you always, to the end of the age.'"

1 **Corinthians 1:9** "God is faithful, by whom you were called into the fellowship of his Son, Jesus Christ our Lord."
1 Corinthians 3:21-23 (1-23) "So let no one boast in men. For all things are yours, whether Paul or Apollos or Cephas or the world or life or death or the present or the future – all are yours, and you are Christ's, and Christ is God's."

3. **John 17:1-3 (see also John 17 whole chapter)** "When Jesus had spoken these words, he lifted up his eyes to heaven, and said, 'Father, the hour has come; glorify your Son that the Son may glorify you, since you have given him authority over all flesh, to give eternal life to all whom you have given him. And this is eternal life, that they know you the only true God, and Jesus Christ whom you have sent.'"
John 17:17-20 (see also John 17 whole chapter) "Sanctify them in the truth; your word is truth. As you sent me into the world, so I have sent them into the world. And for their sake I consecrate myself, that they also may be sanctified in truth. I do not ask for these only, but also for those who will believe in me through their word."

4. **John 20:21-23** "Jesus said to them again, 'Peace be with you. As the Father has sent me, even so I am

sending you.' And when he had said this, he breathed on them and said to them, 'Receive the Holy Spirit. If you forgive the sins of any, they are forgiven them; if you withhold forgiveness from any, it is withheld.'" **Luke 19:10** "For the Son of Man came to seek and to save the lost."

5. **Romans 1:16** "For I am not ashamed of the gospel, for it is the power of God for salvation to everyone who believes, to the Jew first and also to the Greek. **Romans 10:14-17** "How then will they call on him in whom they have not believed? And how are they to believe in him of whom they have never heard? And how are they to hear without someone preaching? And how are they to preach unless they are sent? As it is written, 'How beautiful are the feet of those who preach the good news!' But they have not all obeyed the gospel. For Isaiah says, 'Lord, who has believed what he has heard from us?' So faith comes from hearing and hearing through the word of Christ."

6. **1 Peter 2:9** "But you are a chosen race, a royal priesthood, a holy nation, a people for his own possession, that you may proclaim the excellencies of him who called you out of darkness into his marvelous light."

7. **Ephesians 4:1-7** "I therefore, a prisoner for the Lord, urge you to walk in a manner worthy of the calling to which you have been called, with all humility and gentleness, with patience, bearing with one another in love, eager to maintain the unity of the Spirit in the bond of peace. There is one body and one Spirit – just as you were called

to the one hope that belongs to your call – one Lord, one faith, one baptism, one God and Father of all, who is over all and through all and in all. But grace was given to each one of us according to the measure of Christ's gift." **Matthew 9:35-10:1** "And Jesus went throughout all the cities and villages, teaching in their synagogues and proclaiming the gospel of the kingdom and healing every disease and every affliction. When he saw the crowds, he had compassion for them, because they were harassed and helpless, like sheep without a shepherd. Then he said to his disciples, 'The harvest is plentiful, but the laborers are few; therefore pray earnestly to the Lord of the harvest to send out laborers into his harvest.' And he called to him his twelve disciples and gave them authority over unclean spirits, to cast them out, and to heal every disease and every affliction."

8. **Luke 24:44-47** "Then he said to them, 'These are my words that I spoke to you while I was still with you, that everything written about me in the Law of Moses and the Prophets and the Psalms must be fulfilled.' Then he opened their minds to understand the Scriptures, and said to them, 'Thus it is written, that the Christ should suffer and on the third day rise from the dead, and that repentance and forgiveness of sins should be proclaimed in his name to all nations, beginning from Jerusalem.'" **Ephesians 2:8-9** "For by grace you have been saved through faith. And this is not your own doing; it is the gift of God, not a result of works, so that no one may boast." **1 Corinthians 1:18-31** "For the word of the cross is folly to those who are perishing, but to us who are being saved

it is the power of God. For it is written, 'I will destroy the wisdom of the wise, and the discernment of the discerning I will thwart.' Where is the one who is wise? Where is the scribe? Where is the debater of this age? Has not God made foolish the wisdom of the world? For since, in the wisdom of God, the world did not know God through wisdom, it pleased God through the folly of what we preach to save those who believe. For Jews demand signs and Greeks seek wisdom, but we preach Christ crucified, a stumbling block to Jews and folly to Gentiles, but to those who are called, both Jews and Greeks, Christ the power of God and the wisdom of God. For the foolishness of God is wiser than men, and the weakness of God is stronger than men. For consider your calling, brothers: not many of you were wise according to worldly standards, not many were powerful, not many were of noble birth. But God chose what is foolish in the world to shame the wise; God chose what is weak in the world to shame the strong; God chose what is low and despised in the world, even things that are not, to bring to nothing things that are, so that no human being might boast in the presence of God. And because of him you are in Christ Jesus, who became to us wisdom from God, righteousness and sanctification and redemption, so that, as it is written, 'Let the one who boasts, boast in the Lord.'"

9. **Matthew 16:17-19** "And Jesus answered him, 'Blessed are you, Simon Bar-Jonah! For flesh and blood has not revealed this to you, but my Father who is in heaven. And I tell you, you are Peter, and on this rock I will build my church, and the gates of hell shall not prevail against it.

I will give you the keys of the kingdom of heaven, and whatever you bind on earth shall be bound in heaven, and whatever you loose on earth shall be loosed in heaven.'"

10. **John 15:12-13** "This is my commandment, that you love one another as I have loved you. Greater love has no one than this, that someone lay down his life for his friends."
2 Corinthians 5:18-20 "All this is from God, who through Christ reconciled us to himself and gave us the ministry of reconciliation; that is, in Christ God was reconciling the world to himself, not counting their trespasses against them, and entrusting to us the message of reconciliation. Therefore, we are ambassadors for Christ, God making his appeal through us. We implore you on behalf of Christ, be reconciled to God."
1 John 4:7-16 (see also 1 John 4 whole chapter) "Beloved, let us love one another, for love is from God, and whoever loves has been born of God and knows God. Anyone who does not love does not know God, because God is love. In this the love of God was made manifest among us, that God sent his only Son into the world, so that we might live through him. In this is love, not that we have loved God but that he loved us and sent his Son to be the propitiation for our sins. Beloved, if God so loved us, we also ought to love one another. No one has ever seen God; if we love one another, God abides in us and his love is perfected in us. By this we know that we abide in him and he in us, because he has given us of his Spirit. And we have seen and testify that the Father has sent his Son to be the Savior of the world. Whoever confesses that Jesus is the Son of God, God abides in him, and he in God. So we have come

to know and to believe the love that God has for us. God is love, and whoever abides in love abides in God, and God abides in him."

11. **Romans 1:16-17** "For I am not ashamed of the gospel, for it is the power of God for salvation to everyone who believes, to the Jew first and also to the Greek. For in it the righteousness of God is revealed from faith for faith, as it is written, 'The righteous shall live by faith.'" **John 5:39** "You search the Scriptures because you think that in them you have eternal life; and it is they that bear witness about me." **John 17:17-19** "Sanctify them in the truth; your word is truth. As you sent me into the world, so I have sent them into the world. And for their sake I consecrate myself, that they also may be sanctified in truth." **Galatians 5:1** "For freedom Christ has set us free; stand firm therefore, and do not submit again to a yoke of slavery."

12. **1 Corinthians 12:4-7, 27 (see also 1 Corinthians 12 whole chapter)** "Now there are varieties of gifts, but the same Spirit; and there are varieties of service, but the same Lord; and there are varieties of activities, but it is the same God who empowers them all in everyone. To each is given the manifestation of the Spirit for the common good... Now you are the body of Christ and individually members of it." **Romans 12:3-5 (see also Romans 12 whole chapter)** "For by the grace given to me I say to everyone among you not to think of himself more highly than he ought to think, but to think with sober judgment, each according to the

measure of faith that God has assigned. For as in one body we have many members, and the members do not all have the same function, so we, though many, are one body in Christ, and individually members one of another."

CHAPTER 8

CONCLUSION AND AN INVITATION

CONCLUSION

The Great Sending, which is centered in and illustrates God's heart for the world and for sending you into the world, is a Scriptural immersion to re-set hearts toward the *Missio Dei,* the sending of God, for the salvation of the world.

Through intentional and intensive study of God's holy Word, God produces in individuals and congregations a heart transformation (re-set) that:

1. understands and applies the great sending of God for the salvation of the world through being justified by grace alone in Christ's sending as the core truth and central to our identities as Christians

2. recognizes the *Missio Dei* as the lens for reading, interpreting, understanding, and applying Holy Scriptures and all its teachings, including the divine means of grace, the Word, and the Sacraments

3. realizes the authority, essence, and nature of the *Missio Dei*

4. understands that human means and practices must be *aligned* to the *Missio Dei*, and are not in and of themselves the *Missio Dei*

Through the 42 *immersion Bible Studies* with commentaries by missional leaders, the *Theological Basis for the* Missio Dei *in Scripture*, and the *Missio Dei Catechism, The Great Sending* is Romans 12:1-2 in action:

I appeal to you therefore, brothers, by the mercies of God, to present your bodies as a living sacrifice, holy and acceptable to God, which is your spiritual worship. Do *not be conformed to this world, but be* **transformed** *by the renewal of your mind, that by testing you may discern what is the will of God, what is good and acceptable and perfect.* (Emphasis added)

The good, acceptable, and perfect will of the *Sending God* is revealed and summarized in John 17:18 and John 20:21-23:

As you **sent** *me into the world, so I have* **sent** *them into the world... Jesus said to them again, "Peace be with you. As the Father has* **sent** *me, even so I am* **sending** *you." And when he had said this, he breathed on them and said to them, "Receive the Holy Spirit. If you* **forgive** *[send away] the sins of any, they* **are forgiven** *[sent away] them; if you withhold forgiveness from any, it is withheld."* (Emphasis added)

INVITATION

The Great Sending is an invitation to subscribe to the twelve mission theses *In Nomine Jesu and Soli Deo Gloria* in the presence of God and all Christendom, reflecting your confession of, conviction of, and commitment to align your life and/or congregation's life to the *sending of God (Missio Dei)* in Christ to and for the world. Accepting the invitation reflects an agreement that God's heart for the world is beating through you.

The baptismal and confirmation vows, the pastor's ordination vow, and Luther's nailing of the 95 Theses are/were a public witness of one's confession, conviction, and commitment. Subscription to the Twelve Mission Theses of the Great Sending can be a public witness for the world today. Through these assertions, we encourage one another.

To make public yours or your congregation's commitment to The Great Sending, please email sent@thegreatsending.org. Your pledge will be "nailed to the Church door."

MISSIOLOGICAL RESOURCES
FOR THE GREAT SENDIING

A THEOLOGICAL BASIS FOR THE GREAT SENDING IN JOHN'S GOSPEL

A Missio Dei Immersion Resource for
Pastors And Congregations

INTRODUCTION

Missio Dei – Is this nothing more than another new and popular term focused on missions?

Apostolic Church – Is this term void of meaning today, nothing more than cold space between thick old sanctuary walls?

Or are *Missio Dei* (God's Sending) and *apostolic* (sending) foundational and scriptural understandings meant to reflect a heart transformation toward a mission-based attitude and Gospel-centered movement? We should expect this very mission-based attitude and Gospel-centered movement as the Christian Church and her members are *sent* by Christ, who was *sent* by the Father into the world, and who together with the Father *sent* the Holy Spirit.

Indeed, *Missio Dei* is the great sending act of God! And *Apostolic* is the sent/sending! The Biblical paradigm for "mission" or "missional" is *Missio Dei* in Latin, which we can translate to *God's Sending*. The Biblical root word is ἀποστέλλω (*apŏstĕllō*), from which we derive the terms *apostle*, *apostolate*, and *apostolic*. *God's Sending* is Gospel and the core Biblical message.

God's powerful Word is loaded with astounding mission passages that focus on the verb "to send." We see the *sending of God* motif at work in:

- John 3:16-17
- John 17:3,18
- John 20:21-23
- Matthew 10:1
- Luke 4:18-19, 43-44
- Luke 9:1-3
- Luke 10:1

These texts, together with all the supporting "send" passages in Scripture, provide a sequential, foundational, and Gospel dynamic of the *Missio Dei.*

It is tempting to superficially reference favorite passages such as Matthew 28:16-20 or Acts 1:8 when we are thinking about the sending act of God. While these are supporting passages for the *Missio Dei,* they are far from the whole story as God intends. For a deep heart-transformative understanding of what it is to be missional or apostolic, it is important to reflect on the *sending*-foundational passages above, without using "the great commission" or "mission" lightly.

While this brief chapter primarily focuses on the words of John 17:18 and 20:21-23, the Gospels of Matthew, Mark, and Luke and the Book of Acts, as well as a few passages in the Epistles, also illustrate the *sending* motif of God at work.

THE MISSIO DEI IS GOD'S DYNAMIC SENDING

To fully understand the meaning of *Missio Dei,* it is important to know that the etymology of "mission" is "send." A Latin translation is *"missio,"* or *"mitto."* Greek translations are ἀποστέλλω *(apŏstĕllō)*, πέμπω *(pĕmpō)*, and ἀφίημι *(aphiēmi)*. Matthew and Luke use ἐκβάλλω *(ĕkballō)* (see Matthew 9:38 and Luke 10:1-3). In the LXX (Septuagint) we see the term ἀποστέλλω *(apŏstĕllō)* for the Hebrew שָׁלַח *(shalach)*. Regardless of the language, the central focus is the same: the heart of the dynamic mission is the *sending* of Christ, the *sending* of the Holy Spirit and of Christ's *sending* the church.

Therefore, it is helpful for laity and clergy alike to nurture a deep appreciation of the *sending* motif. One way to do this is to recognize the meanings of the key Biblical *sending (missio)* Greek words themselves. It is also important to take into account some Hebrew words:

ἀποστέλλω *(apŏstĕllō)* – is an official or authoritative sending, an act of sending *out* (properly on a mission), whether literal or figurative. This word can also use *send*:

- as a *departure* (off, away, forth, out)
- as a *dispatch* (on service)
- *to send* with a commission

Note the root for the word *apostle*, from *apŏstĕllō – a delegate, a messenger, one sent on a mission, an* official *representative;* an apostle (or, more specifically, an *ambassador* of the Gospel). An apostle is officially a *com-missioner* of Christ, a messenger, one who is sent. (See John 17:3, 18; 20:21-23; Luke 4:18-19.) The Hebrew שָׁלַח – *shalach* is found in Genesis 3:23, 45:7-8; Exodus 3:10-15; Leviticus 16:10; Isaiah 6:8, 18:1-2, 48:16, and 61:1-2;

and Jeremiah 1:4-10. See also John 9:7 (*Siloam*).

πέμπω (*pěmpō*) – to *send* or *dispatch* (from the subject view or point of *departure*)

ἀφίημι (*aphiemi*) – to *send forth*

in various applications: *cry, forgive, forsake, lay aside, leave, let* (alone, be, go, have), *omit, put* (or *send*) *away, remit, suffer, yield*;

pardon (figurative): deliverance, forgiveness, liberty, dismissal, remission (or "forgive" – see Matthew 9:5-6; 26:28; John 20:23); *leave* (see Matthew 4:20,22; 19:27,29; John 4:28; Leviticus 16:10; Luke 4:18-19 and Isaiah. 61:1), such as *sending* away sin!

ἐκβάλλω (ěkballō) – to *send away* (forth, out); to *eject* (literal or figurative), or to *exit*. A good example of this word at work meaning *to send out* is in Matthew 9:38, when Christ longs for the *sending* of laborers into his harvest. An example of the word connoting an *exit* would be the exit velocity of a baseball; so should our "exit velocity" be of the Church, from the Church into the harvest field.

The word can also mean:

- to *thrust* or *hurl*
- to *bring forth*
- to *cast* (put forth, cast out, drive out, expel)
- to *leave*
- to *pluck* (pull or take out)

שָׁלַח (*shalach*) – to *send* (away, forth, out, or on an official mission, as in envoys or authorized representatives).

The word can also mean:

- to *leave* (let depart, let loose)
- to *free* (release)

Derivatives include such terms as "weapon," "missile," and "outstretching."

KEY "GREAT SENDING" PASSAGES OF ST. JOHN

For God did not send (apŏstĕllō) *his Son into the world to condemn the world, but in order that the world might be saved through him.* —John 3:17

And this is eternal life, that they know you the only true God, and Jesus Christ whom you have sent (apŏstĕllō). —John 17:3

As you sent (apŏstĕllō) *me into the world, so I have sent* (apŏstĕllō) *them into the world.* —John 17:18

Jesus said to them again, "Peace be with you. As the Father has sent (apŏstĕllō) *me, even so I am sending* (pĕmpō) *you." And when he had said this, he breathed on them and said to them, "Receive the Holy Spirit. If you forgive* (aphiemi) *the sins of any, they are forgiven* (aphiemi) *them; if you withhold forgiveness from any, it is withheld."* —John 20:21-23 (Author's note: As Christ was sent, He sends to send (remit) away sin.)

Besides the focus in John's Gospel and the Resurrection and Ascension sending accounts at the *end* of the Gospel story, we can also compare the key sending words in Luke 4:18-19 spoken by Jesus at the *beginning* of His public ministry (in the light of John 3:17, John 17:3, 18, and John 20:21-23). The verses read:

> *The Spirit of the Lord is upon me, because he has anointed me to proclaim good news to the poor. He has sent me to proclaim liberty to the captives and recovering of sight to the blind, to set at liberty those who are oppressed, to proclaim the year of the Lord's favor.* —Luke 4:18-19

With emphasis and additions, we see in greater context the sending words at work:

The Spirit of the Lord is upon me, because he has anointed me to proclaim good news to the poor. He has sent (ἀποστέλλω) *me* (and I am here) *to proclaim liberty* (aphiemi, which can also mean "release," "freedom," "pardon," or "dismissal") *to the captives and recovering of sight to the blind, to set at liberty* (apŏstĕllō or aphiemi) *those who are oppressed* (apŏstĕllō or to send away the crushed into freedom, release, or deliverance) *to proclaim the year of the Lord's favor.*

"SENDING" IN THE CONTEXT OF JOHN 17:3,18 AND JOHN 20:21-31

As recorded in John 12, Holy Week began with Christ's triumphal entry on the day known as Palm Sunday. John 12 is a good summary of events and words of Jesus from that triumphal entry to the Thursday of Holy Week. The "sending" is highlighted in these words leading up to events that unfolded in the Upper Room (words in bold are for author's emphasis):

*And Jesus cried out and said, "Whoever believes in me, believes not in me but in him who **sent** me. And whoever sees me sees him who **sent** me... For I have not spoken on my own authority, but the Father who **sent** me has himself given me a commandment – what to say and what to speak.*
—John 12:44-45, 49

*Truly, truly, I say to you, a servant is not greater than his master, nor is a messenger greater than the one who **sent** him... Truly, truly, I say to you, whoever receives the one I **send** receives me, and whoever receives me receives the one who **sent** me."* —John 13:16, 20

*But the Helper, the Holy Spirit, whom the Father will **send** in my name, he will teach you all things and bring to your remembrance all that I have said to you.* —John 14:26

*"But when the Helper comes, whom I will **send** to you from the Father, the Spirit of truth, who proceeds from the Father, he will bear witness about me. And you also will bear witness, because you have been with me from the beginning.* —John 15:26-27

*But now I am going to him who **sent** me, and none of you asks me, "Where are you going?" Nevertheless, I tell you the truth: it is to your advantage that I go away, for if I do not go away, the Helper will not come to you. But if I go, I will **send** him to you.* —John 16:5, 7

> *And this is eternal life, that they know you the only true God, and Jesus Christ whom you have **sent**.* —John 17:3

> *For I have given them the words that you gave me, and they have received them and have come to know in truth that I came from you; and they have believed that you **sent** me… that they may all be one, just as you, Father, are in me, and I in you, that they also may be in us, so that the world may believe that you have **sent** me… I in them and you in me, that they may become perfectly one, so that the world may know that you **sent** me and loved them even as you loved me… O righteous Father, even though the world does not know you, I know you, and these know that you have **sent** me.* —John 17:8,21,23,25

An extended study of the "sending" theme of the Gospel would begin with John the Baptist in John 1:6, 33 and 3:28. God's sending for Jesus occurs a total of 35 times in St. John from chapters 3 to 16 (not counting chapters 17 and 20 with 7 more "sending" references in contexts apart from God's sending for Jesus). Three more "sending" passages occur in John 14, 15 and 16, with references to the sending of the Holy Spirit

Intrinsic in "sending" is authority and relationship. There must be a connection between the sender and the sent.

THE SEQUENCE OF *"MISSIO DEI"* IN JOHN 17:18 AND JOHN 20:21-31

The following passages take place between Maundy Thursday and Easter Day evening.

In the Upper Room on the night of Maundy Thursday into the early morning of Good Friday, Christ prayed:

As you sent (apŏstĕllō, or "apostled") *me into the world, so I have sent* (apŏstĕllō) *them into the world.* —John 17:18

Author's note: For the importance of the word "as" here (καθώς or kathōs), *see John 3:16-17 and John 20:21-23.*

God *sent* his beloved son, Jesus, to fulfill what we as infallible human beings could not fulfill ourselves: the salvation of the world through an agonizing death and a triumphant resurrection. We see the triumphant sending of Christ at work in the astonishment of the women at the mouth of the empty tomb, Peter and John's stunned reactions at the news that the body of Jesus was not there, the events that unfolded with the disciples on the road to Emmaus, and Jesus's appearances to His disciples behind locked doors following His resurrection. Luke's account of the empty tomb shows the *sent* Christ at work:

And they found the stone rolled away from the tomb, but when they went in they did not find the body of the Lord Jesus. While they were perplexed about this, behold, two men stood by them in dazzling apparel. And as they were frightened and bowed their faces to the ground, the men said to them, "Why do you seek the living among the dead? He is not here, but has risen." —Luke 24:2-6a

This is Jesus, God's sent One, moving.

Then, behind locked doors on the evening of the Resurrection (Easter) Day, Jesus appears to his disciples. We have already considered John 20:21-23 in a *sending* context, but note here, *after* Christ's death and the astounding realization that not even death can contain Him, how the sending work is five-fold:

Jesus said to them again, "Peace be with you. As the Father has sent (apŏstĕllō *or* misit; gesandt) *me, even so I am sending* (pĕmpō *or* mitto; sende) *you." And when he had said this, he breathed on them and said to them, "Receive the Holy Spirit. If you forgive* (aphiemi) *the sins of any, they are forgiven* (aphiemi) *them; if you withhold forgiveness* (aphiemi) *from any, it is withheld."*

God's great sending (the *Missio Dei*) is at work in five ways here: through the Apostle Jesus; through the eleven apostles, through the Holy Spirit, through all believers and through the sending away of sin (forgiveness).

While He is still with his disciples in the Upper Room, Jesus continues to reveal the *Missio Dei* to them:

> *Then he opened their minds to understand the Scriptures, and said to them, "Thus it is written, that the Christ should suffer and on the third day rise from the dead, and that repentance and forgiveness* (aphiemi, *meaning to pardon or send away) of sins should be proclaimed in his name to all nations, beginning from Jerusalem. You are witnesses of these things. And behold, I am sending* (apŏstĕllō) *the promise of my Father upon you. But stay in the city until you are clothed with power from on high." —Luke 24:45-49*

One week later, Jesus appears to his disciples behind locked doors again. This time, Thomas is present. (See John 20:24-31) John clearly states the *Missio Dei* purpose in verse 31:

... but these are written so that (ἵνα [hina]) *you may believe that Jesus is the Christ, the Son of God, and that* (ἵνα [hina]) *by believing you may have life in his name.*

JESUS' APPEARANCES AND ASCENSION CONTEXT

The third time Jesus appears to His disciples after His resurrection, He finds His disciples by the sea:

> *After this Jesus revealed himself again to the disciples by the Sea of Tiberias, and he revealed himself in this way. Simon Peter, Thomas (called the Twin), Nathanael of Cana in Galilee, the sons of Zebedee, and two others of his disciples were together. Simon Peter said to them, "I am going fishing." They said to him, "We will go with you." They went out and got into the boat, but that night they caught nothing... Jesus said to them, "Bring some of the fish that you have just caught." So Simon Peter went aboard and hauled the net ashore, full of large fish, 153 of them. And although there were so many, the net was not torn. Jesus said to them, "Come and have breakfast." Now none of the disciples dared ask him, "Who are you?" They knew it was the Lord... This was now the third time that Jesus was revealed to the disciples after he was raised from the dead. When they had finished breakfast, Jesus said to Simon Peter, "Simon, son of John, do you love me more than these?" He said to him, "Yes, Lord; you know that I love you." He said to him, "Feed my lambs."... This is the disciple who is bearing witness about these things, and who has written these things, and we know that his testimony is true.* —John 21:1-3, 10-12, 14-15, 24

And Matthew shares Jesus's sending mission in Chapter 28:18-20, which could aptly be considered "The Great Going:"

> *"And Jesus came and said to them, 'All authority in heaven and on earth has been given to me. Go therefore and make disciples of all nations, baptizing them in the name of the Father and of the Son and of the Holy Spirit, teaching them to observe all that I have commanded you. And behold, I am with you always, to the end of the age.'"*

If we compare the "great sending" passage of John 17:18 and 20:21-23 with the "great going" passage of Matthew 28:18-20, we see Jesus's awesome authority and directions to *disciple*, to *baptize*, and to *teach* – all of which are a part of the great sending. His command to "Go" in Matthew 28 can be interpreted in a number of ways: *having gone, going, as you are going, now that you have been sent.*

Finally, Jesus appears with God's sending mission in Luke 24:49-50 and in Acts 1:8 (words in bold are author's emphasis):

> *And behold, I am **sending** (apŏstĕllō) the promise of my Father upon you. But stay in the city until you are **clothed with power from on high**. Then he led them out as far as Bethany and lifting up his hands he blessed them.* —Luke 24:49-50

> *"But you will **receive power when the Holy Spirit has come upon you, and you will be my witnesses in Jerusalem** and in all Judea and Samaria, and to the end of the earth."* —Acts 1:8

THE DYNAMIC APOSTOLIC ESSENTIAL ELEMENTS OF THE GREAT SENDING

Elements essential to the Great Sending include the Sender, the Sent Ones, the Sending Authority, the Leaving, the Going, the Sending Task, the Sending Message, the Sending Purpose, the Sending Target, and the Sending Resources, as outlined:

The Sender

The **Heavenly Father** – John 3:16-17, 4:34; John 17, John 20:21; see also John 12:44-50

Jesus – John 17:18; John 20:21; Matthew 10:5, 16; Luke 9:1-6, 10; 10:1-4

The Son of God Who goes into the world, gets His own hands dirty, leaves the comfort of heaven, descends into a world that for the most part (by our sinful human nature) does not welcome Him but that rejects Him

The Sent Ones

Jesus, the Apostle – John 13:16; 17:3,8 18; 21-25; John 20:21; Hebrews 3:1; Luke 4:18-19; Galatians 4:4-5

The Holy Spirit – John 14:26; 15:26; 16:7; Luke 24:49; Galatians 4:6

The angels – Luke 1:19,26 (Gabriel); see also Hebrews 1:14

The baptized, the disciples, the apostles, the believers – John 13:20; John 17:18; John 20:21; Matthew 10; Luke 9:1-6, 10;

10:1-9; Matthew 28:18-20; 1 Corinthians 3:21-22

As the "image bearer" – all representing Jesus with His authority and in relationship to and with Him

The Sending Authority

The Father –John 3:16-17; John 17:18; 20:21

Jesus – Matthew 7:29; Matthew 10:1; Matthew 28:18; Luke 6:13; Luke 9:1-2; Luke 10:1-3; John 17:2; John 20:21; also see Luke 4:31-44

Note the official authoritative relationship and representation

The Leaving

The disciples leaving their nets and boats

The Israelites leaving Egypt, (not just a physical act of leaving but a mind-set, as well – a leaving of culture, traditions, comfort zone, etc.)

Leaving from behind locked doors – see Matthew 4:22; 10:9-10; Luke 9:3-4; 10:4; John. 4:28; 16:28; John 20:19,26; recall the "exit velocity" metaphor

The Going

Abraham – Genesis 12:1

Disciples – Matthew 10:5-6; Matthew 28:7, 10-11, 19; Luke 9:60

The Sending Task

The "as" (καθώς or kathōs) of Christ's work in the Gospel of John has a bearing on the believer's responsibility (see the use of "as" in John 17:18 and 20:21)

- Key words include "salvation," "life," "bear witness," "utter the Word of God," "do the Father's will," "reap," "that the hearers know," "see and believe," "teach," "glorify God," "bear the truth," "cleanse," "forgiveness," "give peace and eternal life"

The "as" in consideration of Christ's task in other passages also have a bearing on the believer's responsibility

- Matthew 10:7 (see also Luke 24:47) – Key words include "proclaim" and "preach"

- Luke 15 – Key words include "seek" and "search"

- Luke 24:48; Acts 1:8 – Keyword "witness"

- Matthew 28:19-20 – Keywords include "disciple," "baptize," and "teach"

- Matthew 18:15-35 – Keyword "forgive"

- Matthew 16:16 – Keyword "confess"

- 1 Peter 2:9 (see also Luke 9 and 10) – Keywords include "declare," "tell out," and "show forth"

The Sending Message

What God has done – 1 Peter 2:9

Jesus, the sent one with eternal life – John 17

The kingdom of heaven – Matthew 10:7

Repentance and forgiveness – Luke 24:47; John 20:23

Christ's suffering and death – Luke 24:46

Reconciliation and the righteousness of God in Christ – 2 Corinthians 5:18-21

Christ's Resurrection and the resurrection of the dead – Acts 4:10-12; 1 Corinthians 15

The Gospel – Romans 1:16

The Sending Purpose (ἵνα [hina])

That Christ be glorified

To be sanctified in the truth

To have eternal life

To be forgiven

To believe in the sent Christ

The knowing of Jesus, the true God

To be ONE with God, with Jesus and with one another

To be filled with Christ-centered joy

To be kept from the evil one while living in (sent into) the world

See John 17 and John 20:31

The Sending Target (scope, recipient)

Bearing the image of the Sender, going into the world which does not welcome us, getting our hands dirty, leaving our comfort zones, and even being rejected

The world (all people and cultures, all tribes and languages)

The lost where they are (in physical location but also in worldview, in values, in behavior, in doubt, etc.)

See Luke 9:1-6; 10:1-7; 19:10; John 17:18; Luke 24:47; Mark 16:15; Matthew 28:19; Acts 1:8; Revelation 14:6

The Sending Resources

Jesus, who is with us always (Matthew 28:20)

The Holy Spirit, who is the power from on high (Luke 24:49; John 14:26; 15:26; 16:7; John 20:22; Acts 1:8)

The Word of Truth (John 17:17)

The Sacraments (Matthew 28:19; 1 Corinthians 11:23-26)

Prayer, but not a means of grace (Matthew 9:38; Acts 2:42; Acts 12:5)

A New Testament Scriptural Apostolic (Sending)Track

The Apostle Jesus – Hebrews 3:1; John 3:17; Luke 4:18-19, 43-44; John chapters 3-17 and 20

Holy Spirit – Matthew 1:20; Luke 1:35, John 14:26; 15:26; 16:7; Luke 24:49; Acts 1:8

The angels – Luke 1:19,26 (Gabriel); see also Hebrews 1:14

John the Baptist – John 1:6-8, 15, 19-34; 3:22-36

The calling of the twelve disciples – Luke 5:1-11; 6:12-16; Mark 1:14-16; 3:13-19

The training of the twelve disciples, during Christ's three-year ministry

Sending training – Matthew 9:35-10:42; Mark 6:7-12; Luke 9:1-6; 10:1-24

Teaching training – Luke 14:15, 15, 20:9; John 4:27-38

The formal "Great Sending" of the apostles and all Christians – John 17:18; 20:21-23

The sending of the Apostle Paul – Acts 9:15; 13:2-4; 22:21 (also note the sending of Barnabas and others)

Great Sending elements – Matthew 28:18-20; Luke 24:46-49; Acts 1:1, 8; 2

CONCLUSION

The *Missio Dei* is the central thrust of the Gospel, regardless of which translation or in which language one reads Scripture. The driving force of a *sent one* (a *sent* individual or a *sent* Church) is an open and willing heart and mindset under the power of the Gospel and the Great Sending. With a transformed heart, the *great sending of God* takes place squarely within God's apostolic authority in and through Christ's "one holy, Catholic (Christian) apostolic church." It is through the Church and the Christian community of faith and mission that the Holy Spirit does its work. (See Luther's *Large Catechism*, Third Article, paragraphs 61-62 and Robert Kolb's *Book of Concord*, Concordia Publishing House 2000.)

A Sending Creed (based on the Apostle's Creed)

God, the sending Father, the Almighty creator of the cosmos,

Sent His only Son Jesus Christ to be conceived by the Holy Spirit and born of the Virgin Mary. He was sent to proclaim freedom. He then suffered at the hands of many, including Pontius Pilate. He was crucified, died, and buried. Within three days, He descended into hell to proclaim victory and rose to life granting God's righteousness by grace through faith. Forty days later, He ascended to heaven. He now eternally reigns at the right hand of His Father. He is judge of all the living and the dead, and He gives life to all who believe in Him.

After the ascension, the Father and Son sent the Holy Spirit to boldly make and call all followers of Christ to His holy apostolic church. He calls us, a community of believers, who are sent to all people with power and strength, courage, and gifts to proclaim the Good News. As the apostles were sent, people believed. As those people believed, they, too, were sent. As they were sent, now we believe. And as we believe, we are sent. AMEN.

A MISSIO DEI CATECHISM

INTRODUCTION

Why a "Catechism" of the *Missio Dei* (*Sending of God* or *Mission of God*)?

The word "Catechism," based on a Scriptural Greek word, κατηχέω (*katēchĕō*), means to instruct, inform, or teach by word. In Acts18:21, Apollos was orally instructed in the way of the Lord. Galatians 6:6 mentions receiving *instruction* (or being *taught*) in the Word. Acts 21:21 and 24 refer to being *informed*. (See also 1 Corinthians 14:19 and Romans 2:18.)

Circa 1528–1529, Dr. Martin Luther produced books of instruction, the *Small Catechism* and the *Large Catechisms*, which were based on a series of sermons and the official visitation of the churches. The catechisms were to instruct and aid pastors, heads of households, and laity to know, understand, and apply God's Word. Luther very much wanted the people of his day to live and practice Biblical truths. His emphasis was teaching the 5 or 6 chief parts of Christian doctrine through basic Christian instruction. This led to him asking simple questions such as, "What is this?" How does this happen?" "What does this mean?" You might recognize these as typical catechism questions today.

The *Missio Dei Catechism* is a handbook of sorts to aid pastors and laity in knowing, understanding, and applying the *sending of God*. The *Missio Dei* is the lens through which Christians should read and interpret God's Word *and* the world – the lens for both the *Word-view* and the *worldview* – all for the being and doing of God's sending, the *Missio Dei*.

Luther's catechisms were highly influential in carrying out the Reformation. His work played a major role in encouraging immersion in God's word, reforming and transforming pastors and congregations to more clearly understand the mission of God. Today, a *Missio Dei Catechism* can similarly encourage believers to be compelled by Christ's love, and to no longer to live for themselves, but to be a new "sent" creation in Christ and His mission authority. In short, this catechism is a resource for Christians to immerse themselves in the *Missio Dei*.

We live in a world that is distressed and scattered, "as sheep without a shepherd," (Mark 6:34). We live amid a growing lack of understanding not only of the *Missio Dei*, but of Scripture itself. How well do you know the Bible? How well does your neighbor know the Bible? All in all, we as a society (at least in the United States) are reading the Bible less, attending church and church functions less and volunteering for activities and missional practices less. The *Missio Dei Catechism* can be used extensively in Christian congregations as a focus-tool for immersion in, revival of, and reset to a Christ-mission (Christ-sending) epiphany. It can be used as a core movement alongside and accompanying a church body's catechism, such as *Luther's Small Catechism* (not ever replacing or devaluing it), which together with his *Large Catechism* is included in the *Confessions of the Evangelical Lutheran Church*. Other resources such as the Apostle's Creed and the Office of the Keys are also useful in broadening an understanding of the *Missio Dei*.

Enjoy a ground-breaking but Scriptural and catechetical understanding of the *Missio Dei!*

As the Father has sent me, I am sending you.
—*John 20:21*

INSTRUCTION (CATECHISM) IN THE *MISSIO DEI*

I. WHAT IS THE *MISSIO DEI*?

From the outset, *mission* must be distinguished from *missions*. *Mission* refers to the mission of God (the *Missio Dei*), the *sending of God*, His *sending* nature and function to rescue the lost world. By contrast, *missions* refers to places, scope, activities, endeavors, needs, forms, or practices. *Mission* has historically been confused with foreign or domestic *missions*, which can encompass a subsidized congregation, a field or geographical area, a budget, an agency, physical buildings and even church planting.

Foreign *missions* and *missionaries* have been wrongly used as the "bullet" for giving, meeting a "mission budget" or motive for stewardship and confusing *missions* with *mission*. While *missions* may help facilitate the *Mission of God*, they are not in and of themselves the Mission of God.

Out of God's love for the fallen world and by His gracious initiative, God *sent* His Son, Jesus Christ to save the lost world that was incapable of saving itself. This is the *Missio Dei*, the *mission* rescue act of God. The *Missio Dei* centers on the *sending* of Jesus, who in turn *sends* believers into the world and who, together with the Father, *sent* the Holy Spirit to empower God's people to receive and proclaim the Gospel and participate in God's mission to save the lost.

The Gospel of Christ is centered in the *sending of God* (*Missio*

Dei) for our salvation.

(To learn more about the *Missio Dei*, refer to the Lutheran Church—Missouri Synod's *A Theological Statement of Mission*, published by the Commission on Theology and Church Relations in 1991.)

The *Missio Dei* is GOD'S [GREAT] SENDING!

1. *John 3:16 For God so loved the world, that he gave his only Son, that whoever believes in him should not perish but have eternal life.*

2. *John 4:34 Jesus said to them, "My food is to do the will of him who sent me and to accomplish his work."*

3. *John 17:1-3 When Jesus had spoken these words, he lifted up his eyes to heaven, and said, "Father, the hour has come; glorify your Son that the Son may glorify you, since you have given him authority over all flesh, to give eternal life to all whom you have given him. And this is eternal life, that they know you the only true God, and Jesus Christ whom you have sent."*

4. *John 17:18 As you sent me into the world, so I have sent them into the world.*

5. *John 20:21-23 Jesus said to them again, "Peace be with you. As the Father has sent me, even so I am sending you." And when he had said this, he breathed on them and said to them, "Receive the Holy Spirit. If you forgive the sins of any, they are forgiven them; if you withhold forgiveness from any, it is withheld."*

6. *Luke 24:45-49 Then he opened their minds to understand*

the Scriptures, and said to them, "Thus it is written, that the Christ should suffer and on the third day rise from the dead, and that repentance and forgiveness of sins should be proclaimed in his name to all nations, beginning from Jerusalem. You are witnesses of these things. And behold, I am sending the promise of my Father upon you. But stay in the city until you are clothed with power from on high."

II. WHAT ARE THE ROOT MEANINGS OF THE WORDS *MISSIO* AND *DEI*?

"Missio" is Latin for the Biblical English word "mission," which is based on the original Greek word for *"send," "sending,"* and *"sent."* The Greek root word, ἀποστέλλω (*apŏstĕllō*, or an official or authoritative sending and authoritative representation), is best translated as "apostolic," "apostolate" or "apostle." Therefore, *Missio* is the same as "send," "apostolate," and "mission." The Hebrew word (שָׁלַח – *shalach*) for "mission" or "send" is translated "apostolic/apostolate/apostle" in the Septuagint (The Old Testament translated into Greek) with the same basic meaning of *sending away* on official business or mission.

To understand the main biblical word for mission (*send,*) three other *sending* root words in the Bible are used in the context of the main apostolic word to help understand the depth of the biblical *sending* motif. One is πέμπω (*pĕmpō*) (*sending* from the subject view or point of departure). Another is ἀφίημι (*aphiēmi*, the main word for the biblically translated word forgiveness, thus a *sending* away of sins, a remission of sins, a release, and this Greek word is also translated leave/leaving/left). One other *sending* word to consider is ἐκβάλλω (*ĕkballō*) (thrust [sending away with velocity] as thrusting the laborers into the harvest field in Matthew 9:38).

Dei is Latin for "divinity" and stands for God the Father, Son and Holy Spirit, the source, authority, and resource of the "sending."

"*Missio Dei*" then is

- The *sending of* God (God is a *sending* God)

- The *sending by* God the Father of Christ into the world

- The *sending by* God the Father and the Son of the Holy Spirit

- The *sending by* Christ of the community of Christ-believers into the world

- The *sending away* of sin by God through Christ

7. **Luke 4:18-19** *The Spirit of the Lord is upon me, because he has anointed me to proclaim good news to the poor. He has sent (ἀποστέλλω, apŏstĕllō) me to proclaim liberty ἀφίημι (aphiēmi) to the captives and recovering of sight to the blind, to set at liberty those who are oppressed (ἀποστέλλω [apŏstĕllō] and ἀφίημι (aphiēmi)), to proclaim the year of the Lord's favor.*

8. **John 20:21-23** *Jesus said to them again, "Peace be with you. As the Father has sent (ἀποστέλλω or apŏstĕllō) me, even so I am sending (πέμπω or pĕmpō) you." And when he had said this, he breathed on them and said to them, "Receive the Holy Spirit. If you forgive ἀφίημι (aphiēmi)*

the sins of any, they are forgiven ἀφίημι *(aphiēmi) them; if you withhold forgiveness from any, it is withheld."*

9. *Leviticus 16:9-10 And Aaron shall present the goat on which the lot fell for the* LORD *and use it as a sin offering, but the goat on which the lot fell for Azazel shall be presented alive before the* LORD *to make atonement over it, that it may be sent away (*שִׁלַּח *– shalach/LXX:* ἀποστέλλω, *apŏstĕllō) into the wilderness to Azazel.*

III. HOW DOES THE PHRASE "CHRIST-APOSTOLIC AUTHORITY" EXPLAIN THE *MISSIO DEI*?

God's mission is centered in Christ, the divine Apostle (Hebrews 3:1), who was the *Sent One*. In that apostolate (office of sending), He was given the authority to go into the world to be flesh of our flesh to rescue mankind. Through His gracious work, Christ was given the authority to give forgiveness and eternal life. Christ confers His apostolic (sending) authority to all believers to participate in His mission of proclaiming the Gospel to the world. In the great sending (apostolate) of God, all baptized believers in Christ are given the authority to proclaim the authority of Christ over all flesh, the world, sin, death, and the devil.

10. *John 17:2 ...since you have given him authority over all flesh, to give eternal life to all whom you have given him.*

11. *Matthew 7:28-29 And when Jesus finished these sayings, the crowds were astonished at his teaching, for he was teaching them as one who had authority, and not as their scribes.*

12. *Matthew 9:6 "But that you may know that the Son of*

> *Man has authority on earth to forgive sins" – he then said to the paralytic — "Rise, pick up your bed and go home."*

13. *Matthew 28:18-19 And Jesus came and said to them, "All authority in heaven and on earth has been given to me. Therefore go and make disciples of all nations, baptizing them in the name of the Father and of the Son and of the Holy Spirit."*

14. *John 10:17-18 For this reason the Father loves me, because I lay down my life that I may take it up again. No one takes it from me, but I lay it down of my own accord. I have authority to lay it down, and I have authority to take it up again. This charge I have received from my Father.*

IV. WHY WAS AND IS THE *MISSIO DEI* (SENDING OF GOD) NEEDED?

The death, decay, destruction, and corruption of the institutional human-ordered Church is in direct proportion to its failing mission health, failure to repent and bear the fruit of participating in the *Missio Dei*. The church needs to repent, be converted and be saved from its selfish war. It can no longer face inward and be an end unto itself. True humility and repentance will lead the church to a commitment, a heart transformation. This is the re-set, renewal, and return to God's *Missio Dei*, His great sending.

Beginning with Adam and Eve, everyone has rebelled against God. Everyone has broken the relationship with Him and has been filled with wickedness and disobedience. Mankind sinned and continues to sin against God's will. We are all guilty and deserve punishment. Because of the reality of sin and its consequence, we all deserve eternal damnation. Our broken relationship with God also manifests itself in broken relationships between one another in society, in families, and in the Christian family, the visible church. Mankind and the church urgently needed and still needs the great *sending* of God for rescue and redemption, and for the restoration of relationships!

The church needs the *Missio Dei* itself to exist for others. Only when God's great sending lives within us can we *go* into the world *for* Him. We do not live for ourselves while we wait for others to recognize God's gifts; we cannot embody a "come to us" attitude and continue on with our own lives. Instead, Christ calls us into the world as apostolates, sending us always beyond and outside of ourselves.

15. **Romans 3:9-20** *What then? Are we Jews any better off? No, not at all. For we have already charged that all, both Jews and Greeks, are under sin, as it is written:*

"None is righteous, no, not one; no one understands; no one seeks for God. All have turned aside; together they have become worthless; no one does good, not even one."
"Their throat is an open grave; they use their tongues to deceive."
"The venom of asps is under their lips."
"Their mouth is full of curses and bitterness."
"Their feet are swift to shed blood; in their paths are ruin and misery, and the way of peace they have not known."
"There is no fear of God before their eyes."

Now we know that whatever the law says it speaks to those who are under the law, so that every mouth may be stopped, and the whole world may be held accountable to God. For by works of the law no human being will be justified in his sight, since through the law comes knowledge of sin.

(For further study, see "The Ten Commandments" and "Close of the Commandments," *Luther's Small Catechism*.)

V. WHAT ARE THE ESSENCE AND ESSENTIALS OF THE GREAT SENDING AND CHRIST-APOSTOLIC AUTHORITY?

SENDER – Jesus did not send Himself! He did not presume the mission Himself without His Father. God the Father sent Him and in that sending, Christ was given authority. Nor did the Holy Spirit presume the mission Himself. The Sender of the Holy Spirit was God the Father and the Son Jesus. Individual believers and the community of faith do not ascribe their mission unto themselves. Their Sender is Christ, who gives authority in His sending of the believers to be co-heirs and co-associates with Him in His mission to the world. The Sender is the initiator!

THE SENT – Jesus was a sent one and the recipient of authority; the Holy Spirit was a sent one and authorized; those who are baptized into Christ are sent ones by Jesus and are granted authority to go into the world with the Gospel.

THE SENDING NATURE (THE FULL CHARACTER AND SIGNIFICANCE OF "*SENDING*")

- An official act or an official function

- "Sending" is, in its essence, the granting of authority

- The Sender is authorizing an official representation of the Sender

- Sending always involves relationship between the sender and sent

- Sending always requires the sacrifice of *leaving* (as Jesus *left* His heavenly home for earth, the disciples left their nets and boats, and the Samaritan woman left her water pot)

- Authorized sending always requires the sacrifice of *going* (see Matthew 28:19 – "as you go")

- Sending always is the giving of an authorized task, such as Christ's rescue mission and the believers or disciples proclaiming the Gospel, witnessing, etc. (see Luke 24:47-49 and Acts 1:8)

- Sending always involves an authorized message such as reconciliation through Christ alone, the Gospel message (2 Corinthians 5:14-21)

- The sending always involves the providing of resources, such as the power of the Holy Spirit (John 20:22), the consistent presence of Jesus (Matthew 28:20), the Word, and prayer

- A core ingredient of sending is its purpose, God's ἵνα *(hina, so that)*, such as forgiveness, eternal life, unity with and in Christ, salvation, know God's love, believe, etc.

- A final and necessary essential of being sent is the recipient or target, the audience – that is, the world, every tribe, language, nation, and all people living on earth

16. *John 20:21-23 Jesus said to them again, "Peace be with you. As the Father has sent me, even so I am sending you." And when he had said this, he breathed on them and said to them, "Receive the Holy Spirit. If you forgive the sins of any, they are forgiven them; if you withhold forgiveness from any, it is withheld."*

17. *Galatians 4:4-5 But when the fullness of time had come, God sent forth his Son, born of woman, born under the law, to redeem those who were under the law, so that we might receive adoption as sons.*

18. *Hebrews 2:14 Since therefore the children share in flesh and blood, he himself likewise partook of the same things, that through death he might destroy the one who has the power of death, that is, the devil.*

19. *Hebrews 3:14 For we have come to share in Christ, if indeed we hold our original confidence firm to the end.*

20. *1 Corinthians 1:9 God is faithful, by whom you were called into the fellowship of his Son, Jesus Christ our Lord.*

21. *Matthew 9:6 "But that you may know that the Son of Man has authority on earth to forgive sins" — he then said to the paralytic — "Rise, pick up your bed and go home."*

22. *John 20:31 But these are written so that you may believe that Jesus is the Christ, the Son of God, and that by believing you may have life in his name.*

23. *2 Corinthians 5:14-21* *For the love of Christ controls us, because we have concluded this: that one has died for all, therefore all have died; and he died for all, that those who live might no longer live for themselves but for him who for their sake died and was raised. From now on, therefore, we regard no one according to the flesh. Even though we once regarded Christ according to the flesh, we regard him thus no longer. Therefore, if anyone is in Christ, he is a new creation. The old has passed away; behold, the new has come. All this is from God, who through Christ reconciled us to himself and gave us the ministry of reconciliation; that is, in Christ God was reconciling the world to himself, not counting their trespasses against them, and entrusting to us the message of reconciliation. Therefore, we are ambassadors for Christ, God making his appeal through us. We implore you on behalf of Christ, be reconciled to God. For our sake he made him to be sin who knew no sin, so that in him we might become the righteousness of God.*

(For further study, see the Second and Third Articles, the Apostle's Creed, and the Office of the Keys, *Luther's Small Catechism.*)

VI. HOW IMPORTANT IS KNOWING, UNDERSTANDING AND APPLYING THE *MISSIO DEI* ESSENTIALS?

If the sent ones fail to participate in God's *Missio Dei* essentials, they should expect disaster and eternal consequences. Neglecting

God's *Missio Dei* leads to chaos and rebellion. This is poignantly illustrated in Israel's failure as recorded in Judges 2:1-3 (see also Ezekiel 33).

Note how each one of the sending essentials was carried out by Christ. Christ did not fail God, His Father who sent Him. Note how each of the essentials was executed by the Holy Spirit, who also did not fail the Senders – God the Father and God the Son.

How important it is then, that the sent believers know, understand, and apply who they are in Christ! They are given a divine authority to represent Jesus. They are given the power and love of God to leave their comfort zones and go with the Gospel of Christ into the world with its diverse and ever-changing cultures, languages, social structures, relationships, values, beliefs, and world views!

24. *John 17:15-19 I do not ask that you take them out of the world, but that you keep them from the evil one. They are not of the world, just as I am not of the world. Sanctify them in the truth; your word is truth. As you sent me into the world, so I have sent them into the world. And for their sake I consecrate myself, that they also may be sanctified in truth.*

25. *Judges 2:1-3 Now the angel of the* LORD *went up from Gilgal to Bochim. And he said, "I brought you up from Egypt and brought you into the land that I swore to give to your fathers. I said, 'I will never break my covenant with you, and you shall make no covenant with the inhabitants of this land; you shall break down their altars.'* **But you have not obeyed my voice.** *What is this you have done? So*

now I say, I will not drive them out before you, but they shall become thorns in your sides, and their gods shall be a snare to you" (emphasis mine).

VII. WHAT IS THE SIGNIFICANCE OF THE GREAT SENDING IN JOHN 17:18 AND JOHN 20:21-23?

(Participants should work together to develop answers to these Catechism questions, based on the verses from John below)

- What is the significance of "as" [καθώς *(kathōs)*]?
- Who and what is the significance of the "you" ["Father"]?
- Who and what the significance of the "me" and "I also"?
- What is the significance of "send," and "sent" (ἀποστέλλω or *apŏstĕllō;* πέμπω or *pĕmpō*)?
- Who and what the significance of the "them" ["you"] and the meaning and application?
- What is the significance of the "world" (κόσμος, *cosmos*), the why, the what, the who, and the how?

26. **John 17:18** *As you sent me into the world, so I have sent them into the world.*

27. **John 20:21-23** *Jesus said to them again, "Peace be with you. As the Father has sent me, even so I am sending you." And when he had said this, he breathed on them and said to them, "Receive the Holy Spirit. If you forgive the sins of any, they are forgiven them; if you withhold forgiveness from any, it is withheld."*

VIII. WHAT IS THE SIGNIFICANCE OF THE GREAT SENDING IN JOHN 17:18 AND JOHN 20:21-23 IN LIGHT OF THE ENTIRE GOSPEL OF JOHN?

(Participants are encouraged to read the full Gospel of John and then work together to answer these Catechism questions)

- How does the use of "sent," "send," and "sending" (ἀποστέλλω or *apŏstĕllō*) in John 17 (seven times) and 20:21 and the whole Gospel of John (read and mark the countless times) shed light on Christ-Apostolic authority?

- How does the use of "world" (κόσμος or *cosmos*) in John 17 alone (eighteen times) and the whole Gospel of John (read and mark the countless times) shed light on Christ-Apostolic authority?

- How does the use of "that," and "so that" (ἵνα, *hina*—*in order that, denoting the [mission] purpose or the result*) in John 17 (eighteen times) and the whole Gospel of John (114 times) shed light on the purpose of Christ-Apostolic authority? (Note: the use of "that" and "so that" appears a total of 570 times throughout the New Testament.)

- How does the use of "as," and "just as" (καθώς or *kathōs*) in John 17 and the whole Gospel of John explain Christ-Apostolic authority? (Hint: see John 13:14-16,34; 15:4,9-13; and Ephesians 4:32; 5:1.)

IX. WHAT IS THE SIGNIFICANCE OF "ONE HOLY CHRISTIAN APOSTOLIC CHURCH" IN LIGHT OF THE *MISSIO DEI* IN JOHN 17?

For centuries, the Christian community of faith and mission has confessed *one holy Christian (catholic) apostolic church* in the Nicene Creed. This reflects the *Missio Dei.*

Oneness. Christ's High Priestly prayer in John 17 makes it clear that the church is *one.* The assembly of believers all over the world are all one in Christ. All Christians are members one of another. We are all one in the Body of Christ. Christ alone has created this oneness, or unity. There is an order to being sent into the world in John 17:18; both believers and those to whom believers are sent become one with Christ and with one another. *Oneness* does not come through having unity of church polity, structures, or agreement in traditions, rites, or ceremonies, nor does it come through willing collaboration in church functions, activities, or building or property enterprises. Jesus prays "that they may be one *as we [the Father and Jesus] are one*" (vs. 11 and 22).

Holiness. The confession also reflects that the one assembly is *holy,* as described in Christ's prayer ("sanctified" in the High Priestly prayer of John 17), to be protected from the evil one and sanctified (made holy) by the Word of Truth (vs. 16-17). As the oneness of the church is rooted in Jesus Christ, so also is the holiness of the church. Christians are not holy through church polity or piety, rules, traditions, practices, laws, or common arrangements, nor are they holy through mere performance of worship, liturgy, and/or ceremonies. The holy Christ has given

His holiness to His own by the shedding of His holy blood.

Christian. The *Christian* church is based on the centrality of Christ, who with authority gives His people eternal life and the means to know the only true God and Jesus Christ. A Christian is one who, in relationship with Christ, knows Christ and possesses His gifts, His oneness, His holiness, His love, and His presence, all the while being in the world, but not of the world (John 17). The church is *catholic*, or universal, in the saving faith wherever the Gospel is preached.

Apostolic. The church is *apostolic*. That means it is a *sent* church. It is also therefore a missionary church (John 17:18). Related root words to "apostolic" are mentioned seven times in John 17. Basing its life on the teachings of the Apostle Jesus Christ Himself, the church is sent into the world while not being of the world. The apostolic church *leaves, goes,* and *takes* the Gospel to the world. The apostolic church has the authority of Christ Himself, just as the Apostles, who were the immediate sent ones of Christ, to proclaim and live the Good News in order that people trust in Jesus and be saved. The apostolic church is engaged with, receives, and participates in Christ's sending as it embraces Christ in saving faith.

> 28. *Matthew 28:18-20 And Jesus came and said to them, "All authority in heaven and on earth has been given to me. Go therefore and make disciples of all nations, baptizing them in the name of the Father and of the Son and of the Holy Spirit, teaching them to observe all that I have commanded you. And behold, I am with you always, to*

the end of the age."

29. **1 Peter 2:9** *But you are a chosen race, a royal priesthood, a holy nation, a people for his own possession, that you may proclaim the excellencies of him who called you out of darkness into his marvelous light.*

30. **John 17:20** *I do not ask for these only, but also for those who will believe in me through their word.*

31. **Ephesians 2:19-22** *So then you are no longer strangers and aliens, but you are fellow citizens with the saints and members of the household of God, built on the foundation of the apostles and prophets, Christ Jesus himself being the cornerstone, in whom the whole structure, being joined together, grows into a holy temple in the Lord. In him you also are being built together into a dwelling place for God by the Spirit.*

32. **Ephesians 4:3-6** *...eager to maintain the unity of the Spirit in the bond of peace. There is one body and one Spirit— just as you were called to the one hope that belongs to your call— one Lord, one faith, one baptism, one God and Father of all, who is over all and through all and in all.*

33. **Romans 12:4-5** *For as in one body we have many members, and the members do not all have the same function, so we, though many, are one body in Christ, and individually members one of another.*

34. **1 Peter 2:5** *You yourselves like living stones are being built up as a spiritual house, to be a holy priesthood, to offer spiritual sacrifices acceptable to God through Jesus Christ.*

35. **Acts 2:42** *And they devoted themselves to the apostles'*

teaching and the fellowship, to the breaking of bread and the prayers.

(For further study see the Third Article, The Apostle's Creed, *Luther's Small Catechism.*)

X. WHAT IS THE SIGNIFICANCE OF CHRIST'S PRAYER AND A PRAYING *MISSIO DEI* CHURCH?

Christ prayed the well-known "Prayer in Gethsemane" the night He was betrayed. It's also important to realize that the prayer of John 17 – the whole chapter – was His prayer the night before He was crucified. In His High Priestly prayer, Christ prayed for Himself and His mission, He prayed for His disciples and their participation in His mission, and He prayed for all believers and those "who will believe" through their being sent. The "just as" is an important conjunction in John 17 and elsewhere in Scripture. *Just as* Christ was sent, He sends us. *Just as* Christ loves, He directs us to love. *Just as* Christ serves, He directs us to serve. Just as Christ prayed, He directs us to pray for ourselves, our receiving and participating in His mission, so that all believers and unbelievers may know Christ's love and be saved.

> 36. **Luke 10:1-2** *After this the Lord appointed seventy-two others and sent them on ahead of him, two by two, into every town and place where he himself was about to go. And he said to them, "The harvest is plentiful, but the laborers are few. Therefore, pray earnestly to the Lord of the harvest to send out laborers into his harvest."*

37. *John 17:1* *When Jesus had spoken these words, he lifted up his eyes to heaven, and said, "Father, the hour has come; glorify your Son that the Son may glorify you."*

38. *John 17:20* *I do not ask for these only, but also for those who will believe in me through their word.*

39. *Philippians 4:6* *Do not be anxious about anything, but in everything by prayer and supplication with thanksgiving let your requests be made known to God.*

40. *John 16:23* *In that day you will ask nothing of me. Truly, truly, I say to you, whatever you ask of the Father in my name, he will give it to you.*

41. *1 Timothy 2:1* *First of all, then, I urge that supplications, prayers, intercessions, and thanksgivings be made for all people.*

42. *Matthew 6:10* *Your kingdom come, your will be done, on earth as it is in heaven.*

(For further study see the Lord's Prayer, *Luther's Small Catechism.*)

XI. WHAT IS THE MEANING AND SIGNIFICANCE OF THE "WORLD" IN THE *MISSIO DEI*?

(The participants are encouraged to read all of John 17 and then work together to answer these Catechism questions)

- What is the meaning of the "world?"

- What is the significance of "not of the world?"

- What is the significance of "not taken out of the world?"

- What is the meaning of "sent into the world?"

- What is a similarity between the *incarnation* of Christ and the *incarnation* of the church in the world? What is a difference?

- What is a similarity between the *exegesis (interpretation, explanation)* of the Word and the *exegesis (interpretation, explanation)* of the *world*? What is a difference?

43. **John 3:16-17** *For God so loved the world, that he gave his only Son, that whoever believes in him should not perish but have eternal life. For God did not send his Son into the world to condemn the world, but in order that the world might be saved through him.*

44. **John 17:18** *As you sent me into the world, so I have sent them into the world.*

45. **Mark 16:15** *And he said to them, "Go into all the world and proclaim the gospel to the whole creation."* (Most manuscripts omit this verse even though it is commonly quoted.)

46. **Psalm 90:2** *Before the mountains were brought forth, or ever you had formed the earth and the world, from everlasting to everlasting you are God.*

47. **Matthew 5:13-14** *You are the salt of the earth, but if salt has lost its taste, how shall its saltiness be restored? It is no longer good for anything except to be thrown out and trampled under people's feet. You are the light of the world. A city set on a hill cannot be hidden.*

48. *Matthew 13:38 The field is the world, and the good seed is the sons of the kingdom. The weeds are the sons of the evil one.*

49. *John 16:8 And when he comes, he will convict the world concerning sin and righteousness and judgment.*

50. *1 John 2:15 Do not love the world or the things in the world. If anyone loves the world, the love of the Father is not in him.*

51. *Revelation 12:9 And the great dragon was thrown down, that ancient serpent, who is called the devil and Satan, the deceiver of the whole world — he was thrown down to the earth, and his angels were thrown down with him.*

(For further study, see First Article, Apostle's Creed, *Luther's Small Catechism*.)

XII. SO, WHAT THEN IS THE MEANING OF BEING SENT INTO THE WORLD?

Because it is the object of Christ's redeeming love, the world is on the receiving end of the sending of God and the mission of the church. Being *sent* means that the community of saving faith is fully aware that it is *sent* to more than the church. It is sent to more than simply the land or the earth, the sea or the animals, the plants, or the sky. Being *sent* means more than going to geographical places – nation states, cities, and villages. The primary target of God's love is His created people (*anthropos, homo, mensch, man*). The community of faith is being *sent* into the "world" which was decorated and adorned (κόσμος or *cosmos*) with His created mankind – with families, men, women, and children. This "world," this "decoration," is a humanity that desperately needs to be saved.

The community of faith and mission is committed to being *sent* into the "world" of people who were created in the image of God. God created humankind with spirit, reason, and senses, with ways of thinking and logic, with relationships, with emotions, with language and communication, with actions and interactions, with learning, wisdom, and material things.

The church is sent to a mankind that was created holy and yet is fallen. We are all sinners, lost and condemned, with unbelief, disobedience, and distorted world views, with deviant behavior. We all live in darkness and filth, tribulation and sorrow, under the prince of this world and under God's judgment.

And yet, this fallen and lost world was in the beginning wonderfully created and perfect.

The community of faith cannot let this scare us. We cannot stay comfortably behind locked doors, hiding in self-preservation and fear. We cannot face inward. Rather, Christ calls us to be *immersed* in the fallen world – to know it and study it, to relate to others and to suffer for and with them. He calls us to love this world. All people of the world need love, precisely because they are living in a world of tension that is inescapable because of sin.

52. John 17:14-16 I have given them your word, and the world has hated them because they are not of the world, just as I am not of the world. I do not ask that you take them out of the world, but that you keep them from the evil one. They are not of the world, just as I am not of the world.

53. *John 17:18 As you sent me into the world, so I have sent them into the world.*

54. *1 Corinthians 9:19-23 For though I am free from all, I have made myself a servant to all, that I might win more of them. To the Jews I became as a Jew, in order to win Jews. To those under the law I became as one under the law (though not being myself under the law) that I might win those under the law. To those outside the law I became as one outside the law (not being outside the law of God but under the law of Christ) that I might win those outside the law. To the weak I became weak, that I might win the weak. I have become all things to all people, that by all means I might save some. I do it all for the sake of the gospel, that I may share with them in its blessings.*

55. *Romans 8:17-18 ...and if children, then heirs—heirs of God and fellow heirs with Christ, provided we suffer with him in order that we may also be glorified with him. For I consider that the sufferings of this present time are not worth comparing with the glory that is to be revealed to us.*

56. *Philippians 1:29 For it has been granted to you that for the sake of Christ you should not only believe in him but also suffer for his sake.*

XIII. WHAT IS THE RELATIONSHIP OF THE GREAT SENDING TO THE SENDING OF THE HOLY SPIRIT?

In the great sending of John 20:21-23, Jesus spoke of receiving the Holy Spirit for the mission. In Luke 24:49, Jesus referred to sending the promised "power from on high." In Acts 1:8, Jesus spoke again of the power when the Holy Spirit comes to empower the believers' mission of witnessing to the ends of the earth. In John chapters 14-16, Christ speaks at length about the sending of the Holy Spirit with references such as "Counselor," "Spirit of Truth," "Teacher of all things," and "Guide." The Holy Spirit lives with and in the believers. The Holy Spirit is connected to the Father and the Son and is connected to the church. He is a Divine resource of the *Missio Dei* for the church, through which He speaks and does His work.

57. **Hebrews 9:14** *How much more will the blood of Christ, who through the eternal Spirit offered himself without blemish to God, purify our conscience from dead works to serve the living God.*

58. **Titus 3:5** *He saved us, not because of works done by us in righteousness, but according to his own mercy, by the washing of regeneration and renewal of the Holy Spirit.*

59. **1 Corinthians 6:11** *And such were some of you. But you were washed, you were sanctified, you were justified in the name of the Lord Jesus Christ and by the Spirit of our God.*

60. **John 3:5-6** *Jesus answered, "Truly, truly, I say to you, unless one is born of water and the Spirit, he cannot enter the kingdom of God. That which is born of the flesh is flesh, and that which is born of the Spirit is spirit."*

61. **John chapters 14-16**

(For further study see the Third Article, The Apostle's Creed, *Luther's Small Catechism.*)

XIV. WHAT IS THE GOD-CREATED AND GOD-GIVEN MEANS TO CARRY OUT THE *MISSIO DEI*?

Through the Holy Spirit, the spoken Word of God, Baptism, the Lord's Supper, and the Office of the Keys are the divinely appointed means of grace that create and sustain saving faith in Christ and His merits. The assembly of believers also provides varied earthly means accessing the divine means: practices, programs, and activities. The earthly means must be aligned to the *Missio Dei* and the divine means of grace without mere performance. Believers cannot simply focus on the secondary means and practices, with the words "mission" and "missions" being carelessly used as slogans.

62. *John 20:21-23 Jesus said to them again, "Peace be with you. As the Father has sent me, even so I am sending you." And when he had said this, he breathed on them and said to them, "Receive the Holy Spirit. If you forgive the sins of any, they are forgiven them; if you withhold forgiveness from any, it is withheld."*

63. *John 5:39 You search the Scriptures because you think that in them you have eternal life; and it is they that bear witness about me.*

64. *2 Timothy 3:15-17 ...and how from childhood you have been acquainted with the sacred writings, which are able*

to make you wise for salvation through faith in Christ Jesus. All Scripture is breathed out by God and profitable for teaching, for reproof, for correction, and for training in righteousness, that the man of God may be complete, equipped for every good work.

65. **Romans 1:16** *For I am not ashamed of the gospel, for it is the power of God for salvation to everyone who believes, to the Jew first and also to the Greek.*

66. **Romans 10:8-17** *But what does it say? "The word is near you, in your mouth and in your heart" (that is, the word of faith that we proclaim); because, if you confess with your mouth that Jesus is Lord and believe in your heart that God raised him from the dead, you will be saved. For with the heart one believes and is justified, and with the mouth one confesses and is saved. For the Scripture says, "Everyone who believes in him will not be put to shame." For there is no distinction between Jew and Greek; for the same Lord is Lord of all, bestowing his riches on all who call on him. For "everyone who calls on the name of the Lord will be saved." How then will they call on him in whom they have not believed? And how are they to believe in him of whom they have never heard? And how are they to hear without someone preaching? And how are they to preach unless they are sent? As it is written, "How beautiful are the feet of those who preach the good news!" But they have not all obeyed the gospel. For Isaiah says, "Lord, who has believed what he has heard from us?" So faith comes from hearing, and hearing through the word of Christ.*

67. **Matthew 28:18-20** *And Jesus came and said to them, "All authority in heaven and on earth has been given to me. Go therefore and make disciples of all nations, baptizing them in the name of the Father and of the Son and of the Holy Spirit, teaching them to observe all that I have commanded you. And behold, I am with you always, to the end of the age."*

68. **Acts 2:38-39** *And Peter said to them, "Repent and be baptized every one of you in the name of Jesus Christ for the forgiveness of your sins, and you will receive the gift of the Holy Spirit. For the promise is for you and for your children and for all who are far off, everyone whom the Lord our God calls to himself."*

69. **Matthew 16:19** *I will give you the keys of the kingdom of heaven, and whatever you bind on earth shall be bound in heaven, and whatever you loose on earth shall be loosed in heaven.*

70. **1 Corinthians 10:16** *The cup of blessing that we bless, is it not a participation in the blood of Christ? The bread that we break, is it not a participation in the body of Christ?*

71. **1 Corinthians 11:24-28** *...and when he had given thanks, he broke it, and said, "This is my body which is for you. Do this in remembrance of me." In the same way also he took the cup, after supper, saying, "This cup is the new covenant in my blood. Do this, as often as you drink it, in remembrance of me." For as often as you eat this bread and drink the cup, you proclaim the Lord's death until he comes. Whoever, therefore, eats the bread or drinks the cup of the Lord in an unworthy manner will be guilty concerning the*

body and blood of the Lord. Let a person examine himself,
then, and so eat of the bread and drink of the cup.

(For further study see Baptism, The Lord's Supper, the Office
of Keys, *Luther's Small Catechism.*)

XV. WHAT ESTABLISHES MUTUAL COMMITMENT AND TRUST FOR PARTICIPATING AND SERVING TOGETHER IN THE *MISSIO DEI*?

Participating and serving together as a fellowship of the baptized
begins with a relationship with Jesus and a trust in Him. Once we
are in relationship with Him, He creates in us a trust in and unity
with one another. Christ and His love alone can create a mutual
trust, which exists in His Body, the Church. That creative Christ-
love gives birth to commitment, where we participate and serve
together. To think that trust and commitment is built on a simple
agreeing with one another or collaborating on building projects,
practices, activities or missions, is at best a fleeting hope. It is like
living in the same house but not married and having nothing but a
shallow existence with no mutual trust or unity. As the members
of the Body of Christ embrace Jesus, they embrace His mission
with the fruit of partnering in the One Body with a seminal trust
and unity in Christ. That is, what results in a mutual trust is
squarely built on relationship with Christ.

> 72. *Ephesians 2:8-9 For by grace you have been saved through*
> *faith. And this is not your own doing; it is the gift of God,*
> *not a result of works, so that no one may boast.*

73. *Psalm 51:10-12* *Create in me a clean heart, O God, and renew a right spirit within me. Cast me not away from your presence and take not your Holy Spirit from me. Restore to me the joy of your salvation and uphold me with a willing spirit.*

74. *John 8:31-36* *So Jesus said to the Jews who had believed him, "If you abide in my word, you are truly my disciples, and you will know the truth, and the truth will set you free." They answered him, "We are offspring of Abraham and have never been enslaved to anyone. How is it that you say, 'You will become free'?" Jesus answered them, "Truly, truly, I say to you, everyone who practices sin is a slave to sin. The slave does not remain in the house forever; the son remains forever. So if the Son sets you free, you will be free indeed."*

75. *John 15:1-5* *I am the true vine, and my Father is the vinedresser. Every branch in me that does not bear fruit he takes away, and every branch that does bear fruit he prunes, that it may bear more fruit... Already you are clean because of the word that I have spoken to you. Abide in me, and I in you. As the branch cannot bear fruit by itself, unless it abides in the vine, neither can you, unless you abide in me. I am the vine; you are the branches. Whoever abides in me and I in him, he it is that bears much fruit, for apart from me you can do nothing.*

76. *Romans 12:1-3* *I appeal to you therefore, brothers, by the mercies of God, to present your bodies as a living sacrifice, holy and acceptable to God, which is your spiritual worship. Do not be conformed to this world,*

but be transformed by the renewal of your mind, that by testing you may discern what is the will of God, what is good and acceptable and perfect. For by the grace given to me I say to everyone among you not to think of himself more highly than he ought to think, but to think with sober judgment, each according to the measure of faith that God has assigned.

XVI. WHAT IS THE SIGNIFICANCE OF CONFESSION AND REPENTANCE IN RECEIVING AND PARTICIPATING IN THE *MISSIO DEI*?

- As a treasured people sent to be "a kingdom of priests and a holy nation" (Ex. 19:5-6) to the world, the children of Israel were in constant need of laying their sins on the scapegoat and repenting (Lev. 16:10), to carry out God's mission in the wilderness and in the promised land

- As a shepherd, called to be king representing God, David confessed his sinfulness, repented, and was forgiven, carried out God's covenant and mission, taught and declared God's ways and righteousness (Psalm 51) to the world

- As a prophet sent to unbelieving and wicked Nineveh, Jonah confessed his sin of fleeing; he repented, and being forgiven, carried out God's mission

- As disciples who were locked behind doors for fear on Resurrection evening and again a week later, God's chosen men carried out Christ's great sending with sins forgiven, with Christ's peace, and as Spirit-energized missionaries to the world

Repentance, which is a change of thinking and behavior, and forgiveness of sins (Luke 24:47) is essential for Christ-followers to participate in the *Missio Dei*. Treasured people of God must confess their sins – sins of fleeing, sins of disobedience to God's sending, failures to submit to His authority, sins of apathy, sins of arrogance. Above all, though, believers must receive forgiveness. Are repentance and forgiveness significant in the great sending of God? Yes!

Regarding the *Missio Dei* specifically, our sins of selfishness, fear, and apathy are crying for repentance and forgiveness. The institutional church often fails to participate in the great sending of God because it is blinded by a deceptive devotion – devotion to and passion for maintaining church buildings and scheduling activities. It comes down to the old self of self-interest, self-being and self-doing. The Church cannot participate in God's sending mission if it is wholly focused on itself.

In arrogance, Christians today also can find fault with and dismiss other Christians who are responding to Christ's sending and who are being used as instruments of God's mission but are not considered to have *pure* theology or *pure* "Lutheran" traditions and liturgy. Christians today can be hindered, detracted from, or outright disobedient to God's sending by such arrogance.

Distraction by multi-faceted doctrinal pressure points often tragically consumes God's treasured and sent people. Let it be clear that *doctrine* can deliberately or by default become central instead of the *Gospel*, the Christ-centered *Missio Dei*. In His love, forgiveness, and peace, which transcends all understanding, together with and for the *Missio Dei*, God necessarily and indeed accompanies the sending with teaching – *teaching them to observe all that I have commanded you. And behold, I am with you always, to the end of the age* (Matthew 28:20).

In Isaiah 1, God condemned the hypocrisy of focus on worship performances and formalities of the people. Because their focus was in the wrong place, they disobeyed and violated His will. Yet graciously, in verse 18, we read: *Come now, let us reason together, says the* LORD: *though your sins are like scarlet, they shall be as white as snow; though they are red like crimson, they shall become like wool.*

If there is to be any receiving of and participation in the *Missio Dei*, under the power of God's Word and grace and by the mercies of God, individual Christians and congregations must lay their sins on Christ, the scapegoat, and heed Christ's call: "*Repent for the kingdom of heaven is at hand.*" In Christ, the sent are forgiven, cleansed, and given transformed (changed) hearts, for the sake of the mighty sending of God.

(For further study see the Ten Commandments and the Office of the Keys and Confession, Christian Questions with Their Answers, *Luther's Small Catechism*.)

77. **Leviticus 16:9-10** *And Aaron shall present the goat on which the lot fell for the* LORD *and use it as a sin offering, but the goat on which the lot fell for Azazel shall be presented alive before the* LORD *to make atonement over it, that it may be sent away into the wilderness to Azazel.*

78. **Matthew 4:17** *From that time Jesus began to preach, saying, "Repent, for the kingdom of heaven is at hand."*

79. *Luke 9:49-50* John answered, "Master, we saw someone casting out demons in your name, and we tried to stop him, because he does not follow with us." But Jesus said to him, "Do not stop him, for the one who is not against you is for you."

80. *Luke 18:9-14* He also told this parable to some who trusted in themselves that they were righteous, and treated others with contempt: "Two men went up into the temple to pray, one a Pharisee and the other a tax collector. The Pharisee, standing by himself, prayed thus: 'God, I thank you that I am not like other men, extortioners, unjust, adulterers, or even like this tax collector. I fast twice a week; I give tithes of all that I get.' But the tax collector, standing far off, would not even lift up his eyes to heaven, but beat his breast, saying, 'God, be merciful to me, a sinner!' I tell you, this man went down to his house justified, rather than the other. For everyone who exalts himself will be humbled, but the one who humbles himself will be exalted."

81. *1 John 1:8-10* If we say we have no sin, we deceive ourselves, and the truth is not in us. If we confess our sins, he is faithful and just to forgive us our sins and to cleanse us from all unrighteousness. If we say we have not sinned, we make him a liar, and his word is not in us.

82. *Psalm 51:10-12* Create in me a clean heart, O God, and renew a right spirit within me. Cast me not away from your presence and take not your Holy Spirit from me. Restore to me the joy of your salvation and uphold me with a willing spirit.

83. *Joel 2:12-13* "*Yet even now,*" *declares the* LORD, "*return to me with all your heart, with fasting, with weeping, and with mourning; and rend your hearts and not your garments.*" *Return to the* LORD *your God, for he is gracious and merciful, slow to anger, and abounding in steadfast love; and he relents over disaster.*

84. **Psalm 51:17** *The sacrifices of God are a broken spirit; a broken and contrite heart, O God, you will not despise.*

85. **Matthew 3:8** *Bear fruit in keeping with repentance.*

XVII. WHY AND HOW ARE MISSIONAL PRACTICES ALIGNED TO THE *MISSIO DEI*?

Missional practices, performances, facilities, properties, and arrangements are beneficial aids, which must be aligned to the mission of God. This means that every congregational activity, program, project, and organization must be rooted in the *Missio Dei*. We cannot confuse the actions and activities that *support* the *Missio Dei* as the *Missio Dei*. Such actions and activities are rather supporting elements *of* the *Missio Dei*.

For example, nowhere in the Bible does God say we *must* offer or attend Sunday School. However, in the great going, Christ commands us to make disciples. So, it is well and good for a church to offer a Sunday School program as a way of making disciples. But the Sunday School program itself is not the *Missio Dei*. Sunday School teaching should not simply consist of a lesson or head knowledge, an activity or a craft. Any activity or program that is not rooted in God's sending mission is folly.

Every congregational happening *must* be aligned to Christ and His mission without the activities or practices being the central focus or being the mission.

Any missional practices in a healthy missional congregation will be designed for making Gospel contact, useful for connecting, caring, cultivating, communicating, and community-creating, all with the intention of pointing the focus to Christ's apostolic authority. Thus, it is important for congregations to examine who they are – their whole mission ethos, culture, and behavior.

In order to be missional, a congregation must solidly understand the difference between the sending of God and human-appointed sending practices. The sending practices point to the mission of God but are not by themselves the mission of God.

See above relevant passages.

XVIII. WHAT IS THE IMPORTANCE OF CHRIST-CENTERED LEADERSHIP IN THE EMBRACING OF AND PARTICIPATION IN THE *MISSIO DEI*?

To equip, restore, perfect, or repair (καταρτισμός or *katartismŏs*) God's people for participating in His mission, strong leadership in Christ is required. This leadership flows from a saving faith in Christ and is driven by Christ's love for the world. *Missio Dei* leaders are in relationship with Christ, lead by Christ's example, communicate Christ's power and willingly go in the direction Christ points. Factors essential to Christ leadership include but are not limited to:

- **Self-awareness** (knowing who and whose you are, your strengths and weaknesses, possessing a defined reality (a

282 | The Great Sending

sense for what is real)

- **Generative** (creating, creative, originating, producing, procreating, incarnational)

- **Transitional** (adapting, adjusting, movement or passage; developing with καταρτισμός [*katartismŏs*] – *mending, repairing, restoring, equipping, perfecting, completing*)

- **Transformative** (changing, changed in form, character, or condition; with *katartismŏs*)

- **Collaborative** (relational and connecting, working together)

- **Missional** (always in everything focusing on the Christ-mission, on the mission vision, and not on the system, structure, traditions, institution, or mere performance)

Such Christ-leadership is *dynamic!* Like a flowing stream, it is always living, moving, carrying, refreshing, changing, generating. It is always in transition and always transforming, moving God's people from "here" to "there." The *there* is the being immersed in the *Missio Dei*, receiving and participating in Christ's apostolic authority.

86. *John 7:38 Whoever believes in me, as the Scripture has said, "Out of his heart will flow rivers of living water."*

87. *John 10:1-16 Truly, truly, I say to you, he who does not enter the sheepfold by the door but climbs in by another way, that man is a thief and a robber. But he who enters by the door is the shepherd of the sheep. To him the gatekeeper opens. The sheep hear his voice, and he calls*

his own sheep by name and leads them out. When he has brought out all his own, he goes before them, and the sheep follow him, for they know his voice. A stranger they will not follow, but they will flee from him, for they do not know the voice of strangers. This figure of speech Jesus used with them, but they did not understand what he was saying to them. So Jesus again said to them, "Truly, truly, I say to you, I am the door of the sheep. All who came before me are thieves and robbers, but the sheep did not listen to them. I am the door. If anyone enters by me, he will be saved and will go in and out and find pasture. The thief comes only to steal and kill and destroy. I came that they may have life and have it abundantly. I am the good shepherd. The good shepherd lays down his life for the sheep. He who is a hired hand and not a shepherd, who does not own the sheep, sees the wolf coming and leaves the sheep and flees, and the wolf snatches them and scatters them. He flees because he is a hired hand and cares nothing for the sheep. I am the good shepherd. I know my own and my own know me, just as the Father knows me and I know the Father; and I lay down my life for the sheep. And I have other sheep that are not of this fold. I must bring them also, and they will listen to my voice. So there will be one flock, one shepherd."

88. **Psalm 23:1-6** *The* LORD *is my shepherd; I shall not want. He makes me lie down in green pastures. He leads me beside still waters. He restores my soul. He leads me in paths of righteousness for his name's sake. Even though I walk through the valley of the shadow of death, I will fear no evil, for you are with me; your rod and your staff,*

they comfort me. You prepare a table before me in the presence of my enemies; you anoint my head with oil; my cup overflows. Surely goodness and mercy shall follow me all the days of my life, and I shall dwell in the house of the LORD *forever.*

89. **Hebrews 13:17** *Obey your leaders and submit to them, for they are keeping watch over your souls, as those who will have to give an account. Let them do this with joy and not with groaning, for that would be of no advantage to you.*

90. **Ephesians 4:12-16** *...to equip the saints for the work of ministry, for building up the body of Christ, until we all attain to the unity of the faith and of the knowledge of the Son of God, to mature manhood, to the measure of the stature of the fullness of Christ, so that we may no longer be children, tossed to and fro by the waves and carried about by every wind of doctrine, by human cunning, by craftiness in deceitful schemes. Rather, speaking the truth in love, we are to grow up in every way into him who is the head, into Christ, from whom the whole body, joined and held together by every joint with which it is equipped, when each part is working properly, makes the body grow so that it builds itself up in love.*

91. **Hebrews 13:20-21** *Now may the God of peace who brought again from the dead our Lord Jesus, the great shepherd of the sheep, by the blood of the eternal covenant, equip you with everything good that you may do his will, working in us that which is pleasing in his sight, through Jesus Christ, to whom be glory forever and ever. Amen.*

XIX – WHAT IS THE MOTIVATION FOR PARTICIPATING IN THE *MISSIO DEI*?

How do we motivate ourselves and others to participate in the *Missio Dei*? That is another big question. The answer to this last *Missio Dei* catechism question is essential.

The devil, the world, and our flesh tempt us by trying to deceive or lure us into apathy, anarchy, disobedience, distraction, and preoccupation with self. The devil, the world, and our sinful nature would love nothing more than for Christ's beloved to evade His call, His sending. These sin-filled three love to see members of the faith community weak and tired, to be satisfied with old mindsets and habits.

Is motivation essential for participating in the *Missio Dei?* Yes!

Moreover, one way that evil loves to deceive Christ believers is to motivate them with the law and its curbs and commands, taking the believers' focus off the Gospel. We can be deceived by fear – threats that you will get what is coming to you or threats of God's wrath and judgment on the unbelieving world. We can be deceived by seeming goodness of pure doctrine, piety, volunteerism. These are good things, to be sure, but without the love and mercy of the Gospel, they are meaningless.

Motivation from Christ alone moves believers to participate in His sending (mission) – His love, His work! Yes, *God's sending.* What alone moves the believer is the power of the Gospel – being baptized into Christ. It is Christ's saving relationship with His beloved children – not His directions or commands – that brings about change of heart and life. It is His love, not my love; His grace, not my gratitude; His service, not my service. (Parents, this also applies to the parent-child relationship. Pastors, this applies to the pastor-congregation relationship.)

Biblical examples of being motivated by the law include command- or need-passages. While all of these are strong and wonderful passages in the right context, it is easy to focus on the "do" that we can accomplish through them while forgetting the "done" that has already been accomplished through Christ:

> **Luke 14:23** *And the master said to the servant, "Go out to the highways and hedges and compel people to come in, that my house may be filled.*

> **Acts 16:9** *And a vision appeared to Paul in the night: a man of Macedonia was standing there, urging him, and saying, "Come over to Macedonia and help us."*

> **Matthew 24:14** *And this gospel of the kingdom will be proclaimed throughout the whole world as a testimony to all nations, and then the end will come.*

> **John 10:10** *The thief comes only to steal and kill and destroy. I came that they may have life and have it abundantly.* (Author's note: This passage is interpreted by many to mean good things of education and healing for the deprived of the world – social gospel.)

> **Matthew 28:19-20** *Go therefore and make disciples of all nations, baptizing them in the name of the Father and of the Son and of the Holy Spirit, teaching them to observe all that I have commanded you. And behold, I am with you always, to the end of the age.*

> **Acts 1:8** *But... you will be my witnesses in Jerusalem and in all*

Judea and Samaria, and to the end of the earth.

The Gospel, which is centered in the sending and saving activity of Christ, moves the individual Christian and congregation to participate in Christ's sending! This catechism question ends where it began with Articles I to III, the Gospel essence of *God's sending*, the *Missio Dei*.

92. **John 3:16-17** *For God so loved the world, that he gave his only Son, that whoever believes in him should not perish but have eternal life. For God did not send his Son into the world to condemn the world, but in order that the world might be saved through him.*

93. **John 17:2-3** *...since you have given him authority over all flesh, to give eternal life to all whom you have given him. And this is eternal life, that they know you the only true God, and Jesus Christ whom you have sent.*

94. **John 17:18** *As you sent me into the world...*

95. **Romans 1:16** *For I am not ashamed of the gospel, for it is the power of God for salvation to everyone who believes, to the Jew first and also to the Greek.*

96. **Matthew 9:2,6** *And behold, some people brought to him a paralytic, lying on a bed. And when Jesus saw their faith, he said to the paralytic, "Take heart, my son; your sins are forgiven... But that you may know that the Son of Man has authority on earth to forgive sins" — he then said to the paralytic — "Rise, pick up your bed and go home."*

97. **Luke 19:10** *For the Son of Man came to seek and to save the lost.*

98. *John 10:11 I am the good shepherd. The good shepherd lays down his life for the sheep.*

99. *John 10:14 I am the good shepherd. I know my own and my own know me.*

100. *2 Corinthians 5:18-21 All this is from God, who through Christ reconciled us to himself and gave us the ministry of reconciliation; that is, in Christ God was reconciling the world to himself, not counting their trespasses against them, and entrusting to us the message of reconciliation. Therefore, we are ambassadors for Christ, God making his appeal through us. We implore you on behalf of Christ, be reconciled to God. For our sake he made him to be sin who knew no sin, so that in him we might become the righteousness of God.*

101. *John 1:29 The next day he saw Jesus coming toward him, and said, "Behold, the Lamb of God, who takes away the sin of the world!"*

102. *Matthew 28:18 And Jesus came and said to them, "All authority in heaven and on earth has been given to me."*

(For further study see the Second and Third articles, the Apostles Creed, Baptism, the Lord's Supper, and the Office of Keys, *Luther's Small Catechism.*)

The Great Sending—
God's Heart for the World Beating Through You!

THE CONSORTIUM OF CONTRIBUTORS

The following Preface and Commentary contributors are God's sent representatives, bringing the power of God's Word to each Missio Dei participant. This consortium of missional leaders of The Lutheran Church—Missouri Synod are servants of God sent with God's heart for the world. They have generously provided the Missional Immersion Bible Studies and other content in this initiative for participants of the Great Sending.

Rev. Dr. David H. Benke

Rev. Dr. David H. Benke is the retired President/Bishop of the Atlantic District of the Lutheran Church—Missouri Synod. He represented the eastern half of New York State for the denomination from 1991 to 2015. Ordained into the Holy Ministry in the Missouri Synod in 1972, he has served as Pastor of St. Peter's Lutheran Church in Brooklyn, New York, for over four decades and served as President of the Atlantic District from 1997 to present.

Born and raised in Milwaukee, Wisconsin, Benke is a product of the Lutheran educational system from grade school through graduate school, attending schools in Milwaukee, Fort Wayne, St. Louis, and New York. He received the Doctor of Ministry degree from New York Theological School in 1983. He has received several honorary doctorates, including one from Concordia College, Bronxville, on whose Board of Regents he served for over two decades.

In 2001, following the events of September 11, Benke co-founded the Lutheran Disaster Response of New York, which provided twenty-five million dollars to immigrants and others victimized by the historic terrorist attacks. Lutheran Disaster Response of New York was the agency of choice for the Victims' Families Association and sponsored the Visitors' Center (now the Tribute Center, in Lower Manhattan. The theme, "Engaging the World with the Gospel of Hope", developed on the day of the terrorist attacks, well described Benke's vision.

During his tenure in Brooklyn, Dr. Benke helped initiate and has continued to promote the Nehemiah Plan, which has led to over 4000 single-family homes being built on formerly ravaged inner-city acreage. Dr. Benke enlisted partners through the decades to provide undergirding interest funding for Nehemiah Homes. He currently serves as the President of the National LCMS Housing Support Corporation. He and others are now fighting for anti-displacement measures and deeply affordable housing alternatives in rapidly gentrifying neighborhoods in Brooklyn and other New York City neighborhoods, including the construction of 15,000 affordable senior housing apartments.

In 2017 Benke received the "50 over 50 Award" given by City and State New York for being one of the 50 most influential leaders in New York over the age of 50. He continues to serve as Pastor of St. Peter's, a lively multi-cultural and multi-national congregation.

Benke has served continuously on the Board of Mill Neck Manor School for the Deaf since 1992, and currently is the Chair of the Foundation Board. Mill Neck's mission to serve deaf people locally, nationally and globally lines up with his vision to engage the world with the Gospel of hope.

Benke is happily married to Judy, who retired as Vice President for Church and Community Relations at The Lutheran Care Network, New Rochelle, New York. Judy has most recently served on the Board of Lutheran Immigration and Refugee Service and chairs the board of The Center for Urban Education Ministry. The Benkes live in Oakland Gardens, Queens, where they enjoy driving their retirement sports car on the way to and from New York Mets games.

Rev. Dr. David D. Buegler

Rev. Dr., David Buegler was marked by the cross of Christ on his infant head and heart in Holy Baptism August 18, 1946. Godly parents nurtured him on the family farm in southern Minnesota. He attended college at Minnesota State University, where he received a Bachelor of Science degree. Susan is his bride of over 50 years.

Buegler attended Concordia Theological Seminary in Springfield, Illinois, and served as vicar at Trinity Lutheran Church in Jackson, Michigan. Upon his Seminary graduation and following his ordination into the Holy Ministry on June 16, 1972 at the very church where he was baptized and confirmed, he was called back to his vicarage congregation to serve as their pastor. In Jackson Buegler and his wife were blessed with the birth of two daughters, Kristen and Carol.

Buegler served that first parish until 1980, when he accepted a call to serve St. Paul Lutheran congregation in Napoleon, Ohio. He served St. Paul until 1988, when he was elected District President of the Ohio District of the Lutheran Church—Missouri Synod. After serving three terms, he continued his pastoral ministry by accepting a call to St. Paul Lutheran congregation in Westlake, Ohio, where he served from 1996 to 2003. His full-time professional ministry concluded with five years serving as the Executive Director of the Cleveland Lutheran High School Association.

During his ministry Buegler was awarded two honorary Doctor of Laws degrees from Concordia Universities in Ann Arbor, Michigan, and River Forest, Illinois. He was also elected to serve two terms as one of the Vice Presidents of the Lutheran Church—Missouri Synod. His role as Vice President lasted from 2004 to 2010. He served as guest preacher on *The Lutheran Hour* radio program and is a frequent speaker throughout LCMS congregations.

In addition to serving on dozens of District and Synodical boards, committees and councils, he also served the church on three Blue Ribbon Task Forces on Funding and Structure. He continues to serve his community on Social Service boards, hospital boards, and Community Foundation boards.

Even in retirement Buegler's life is packed with service to church and community. His love for the Book of Revelation has enabled him to teach an overview of the entire book to thousands of people throughout the United States, Nigeria, and India. He has also traveled several times to Puerto Rico and Haiti. All in all, he lives and teaches with a love for stewardship and missions.

Rev. Dr. Jon Diefenthaler

Jon Diefenthaler is a President Emeritus of the Southeastern District of the Lutheran Church—Missouri Synod, having served in that office from 2003 to 2012.

He is currently a Church-Relations Advisor for Lutheran World Relief and an Adjunct Professor at Concordia Seminary St. Louis. He also serves on various boards of directors, including Faith and Work Enterprises in Baltimore, Mid-Atlantic Lutherans in Mission, the Lutheran Historical Conference, and the Lutheran Historical Society–Mid-Atlantic. He is also on the editorial committee of the journal *Lutheran Mission Matters*.

Dr. Diefenthaler was born and grew up in Milwaukee, Wisconsin, and is graduate of Concordia College Milwaukee (1963), Concordia Senior College Ft. Wayne (1965), and Concordia Seminary St. Louis (1969). He also received an M.A. in American History from Washington University St. Louis (1970), and a Ph.D. in American Religious History from the University of Iowa (1976). The subject of his doctoral dissertation was H. Richard Niebuhr, and he has published two books on the work of this 20th century American theologian: *H. Richard Niebuhr: A Lifetime of Reflections on the Church and the World* (1986), and *The Paradox of Church and World: Selected Writings of H. Richard Niebuhr* (2015).

During the course of his career, Dr. Diefenthaler was on the faculty of Concordia Theological Seminary, Springfield (1972–1975), and he served as pastor of Bethany Lutheran Church in Waynesboro, Virginia (1975–1997). He later served as senior pastor of Our Savior Lutheran Church in Laurel, Maryland (1997–2003). As a District President, he was a member of the LCMS Board of University Education (2005–2009), the Commission on Theology and Church Relations (2009–2112), and Vice Chair of the Council of Presidents (2009–2012). In addition, he was a member of the Board of Regents, Concordia College New York (2013–2016), as well as the Board of Directors of Lutheran World Relief (2009–

2012) and the We Raise/Wheat Ridge Foundation (2013–2020).

Dr. Diefenthaler has been widowed two times: Linda Reineck (1994) and Vivi Provine (2018), and he has four children: Andrew (Beth) in Richmond, Virginia; Katie Wiltse (Eric) in Overland Park, Kansas; Lisa Woodson (Tracy) also in Richmond; Heidi Bernardi (Sam) in Valparaiso, Indiana. He has twelve grandchildren. He lives in Columbia, Maryland, where he has been for the past two decades.

Reverend Ken Hennings

Rev. Ken Hennings was born in Ft. Lauderdale, Florida. He graduated from St. John's Lutheran College in Winfield, Kansas, and Concordia Senior College in Ft. Wayne, Indiana, and earned his Master of Divinity degree from Concordia Seminary in St. Louis, Missouri, in 1973.

Hennings's first Call was to Trinity Lutheran Church in Uvalde, Texas. In 1978 he accepted the Call to St. Paul Lutheran Church in Fort Worth, where he served as pastor until 1991. He accepted the Call to serve as the Executive Director of the Board of Mission Administration of the Texas District of the Lutheran Church—Missouri Synod (LCMS) in Austin. He served as Mission and Ministry Coordinator of the Texas District and worked with the Board of Mission Administration in directing the District's mission outreach. In 2006 he was elected President of the Texas District, continuing with the Mission and Ministry Facilitators team to provide leadership for the congregations of the Texas District to "reach the lost, disciple the saved, and care for people... locally and globally." Hennings served as President of the Texas District through August 2018. From 2015 to 2018 he was Chairman of the Council of Presidents of the LCMS.

Hennings served as Chairman of the North American Mission Executives of the LCMS, Chairman of Floor Committee #1 (Missions) for the 2010 LCMS Convention. He has also served as Chairman of the Board of Directors of Lutheran Outdoors Ministry of Texas, Chapter Advisor to Lutherans for Life, Facilitator of the LCMS New Church Development Task Force, Zone Counselor for Lutheran Women's Missionary League (LWML), and as a member of the LCMS Harmony Task Force.

Hennings and his wife, Val, are members of Redeemer Lutheran Church in Austin. They have four children and eight grandchildren: Kim (Eric) Otten, with children Nathaniel, Matthew, and Joanna of Omaha, Nebraska; Rev. Paul Hennings, with children Theo and Toby of Cedar Rapids, Iowa; Rev. Luke (Lisa) Hennings, with children Logan, Caleb, and Grant of Mesa, Arizona; and Erika Hennings of New York, New York.

Rev. Dr. Gerald B. Kieschnick

Dr. Gerald B. (Jerry) Kieschnick served from 2001 to 2010 as president of the two-million-member Lutheran Church—Missouri Synod. Prior to becoming LCMS president, Kieschnick had been president of the Synod's Texas District for 10 years.

Upon completion of his third three-year term as Synod president in 2010, Dr. Kieschnick and his wife, Terry, returned to Texas. There he served as Presidential Ambassador for Mission Advancement at Concordia University Texas from 2011 to 2015) and developed Concordia's Christian Leadership Institute.

In 2016 he returned to the Lutheran Foundation of Texas,

recently renamed Legacy Deo, where he had served from 1986 to 1991. In 2017 he was named Chief Executive Officer of Legacy Deo, which exists to help Christians use God's gifts to create a legacy for family and faith. Its mission is to inspire giving that impacts life forever.

He currently serves as founding member and pastoral advisor of Mission of Christ Network; founding member of Ministry Focus; founding member of Pastor 360; and board member of Driving Hope of Texas.

He has also served as elementary Lutheran school teacher; mission developer; parish pastor; chairman of the LCMS Commission on Theology and Church Relations; and chairman of The International Lutheran Council, comprising presidents and bishops of over 35 worldwide Lutheran church bodies.

During his tenure as national church president, Dr. Kieschnick led a national campaign, *Fan into Flame*, which resulted in gifts of $80,000,000 for national and international mission work.

A native of Houston, Dr. Kieschnick holds degrees from Texas A&M University (Animal Science), where he was a Corps of Cadets Company Commander and member of the Ross Volunteers; Concordia Theological Seminary (Bachelor and Master of Divinity); and Concordia University Texas (Doctor of Laws).

He and Terry, his wife of 50-plus years, have two grown children, one son-in-law, and two grandchildren, all of whom live in Texas.

Reverend Keith Kohlmeier

Rev. Keith Kohlmeier served as a parish pastor for 25 years in the Iowa West District, in Farnhamville and Spencer, and in the Kansas District, in Wichita. He served as President of the Kansas District for twelve years, and as a Vice President for Ministry Support with Lutheran Church Extension Fund for three years before retirement. He has held a number of offices at both District and Synod levels, including a member of the Clergy, Call and Roster Committee of the Council of Presidents, an officer of the Council of Presidents, a member of the Synod Presidents' Council, and a member of the Board of Regents of Concordia Seminary in St. Louis. He has written for numerous publications and in retirement continues to serve through Mission Nation Publishing, as a reviewer for several publications, and as a volunteer for serval agencies of the church.

His wife of 48 years, Marlene, is an R.N. who has served in Oncology, School Nursing, and as a Parish Nurse. Kohlmeier and his wife have three children, Jake (Ali), Jeremy (Cori),, and Emily (Steven), and six grandchildren. Together they have served in short term mission projects in Guinea West Africa and Zacapa Guatemala.

Rev. Dr. David Maier

Rev. Dr. David P. E. Maier was elected President of the Michigan District, LCMS in June 2009. He was re-elected to additional terms in 2012, 2015, and 2018. He was also elected to serve as the Chairman of the Council of Presidents for the LCMS in 2018.

President Maier received his B.A. from Concordia University Ann Arbor with a double major in Biblical Languages and Christian Doctrine. He received his Master of Divinity from Concordia Theological Seminary in Fort Wayne, Indiana.

Maier was awarded an honorary doctorate by St. Peter

Confessional Lutheran Church of South Africa in 2007. He was presented with the Outstanding Alumnus Award in May 2010 at Concordia University, Ann Arbor. In 2012, Concordia University, Ann Arbor, awarded him the Doctorate of Laws Degree in recognition of a lifetime of outstanding leadership and diligent labor in the Lord's Kingdom. Concordia University Wisconsin conferred the honorary degree of Doctor of Letters to Maier in December of 2012.

Rev. Dr. Paul Maier

Rev. Dr. Paul L. Maier is a graduate of Harvard University (MA, 1954), of Concordia Seminary, St. Louis (M.Div., 1955), and of the University of Basel Switzerland (Ph.D., 1957). Since 1958 he served as campus Chaplain to Lutheran students at Western Michigan University, where he also taught as Professor of History from 1960 until his retirement in 2011. He served as a four-term Vice President of the LCMS and has published numerous books. Seven of his books he has written for children.

After completing *A Man Spoke, The World Listened,* the biography of his father, Dr. Walter A. Maier, the founding speaker of *The Lutheran Hour,* Dr. Maier turned to writing documentary novels: *Pontus Pilot* and *Flames of Rome.* These were followed by a fiction trilogy: *Skeleton in God's Closet, More Than a Skeleton,* and *Constantine Codex. First Christmas* and *First Easter* are included in *Fullness of Time.* Maier's latest book is *The Genuine Jesus: Fresh Evidence from History and Archeology.*

Maier has also recorded four seminars on DVD focusing on Jesus, St. Paul, the Early Church, and contemporary Christianity. He conducts Mediterranean cruises to the Bible Lands.

Rev. Dr. Dale A Meyer

Dr. Dale A. Meyer is president emeritus and professor emeritus of Concordia Seminary, St. Louis. Meyer retired in 2020 after 15 years as Seminary president. He first joined the faculty at Concordia Seminary as a guest instructor, serving from 1979 to 1981. He then served as an assistant professor from 1981 to 1984. In 2001, he rejoined the faculty and served as professor of Practical Theology in addition to his role as president.

He previously served as the Gregg H. Benidt Memorial Chair in Homiletics and Literature (2001–2005). He served as the interim president (2004–2005) and became the tenth president of Concordia Seminary in 2005.

After earning a Master of Divinity from Concordia Seminary (1973), Meyer earned a master's degree (1974) and a doctorate (1986) in classical languages from Washington University in St. Louis. He completed his bachelor's degree (1969) at Concordia Senior College in Fort Wayne, Indiana. He also is the recipient of an honorary Doctor of Divinity (1993) from Concordia Theological Seminary in Fort Wayne.

Meyer's first call was as pastor of St. Salvator Lutheran Church in Venedy, Illinois., and St. Peter Lutheran Church in New Memphis, Illinois, where he served from 1974 to 1981. After his tenure as a guest instructor at Concordia Seminary (1979–1981), he served as an assistant professor, teaching classes in New Testament and homiletics, and as the director of Resident Field Education (1981–1984). He went on to become senior pastor at Holy Cross Lutheran Church in Collinsville, Illinois, from 1984 to 1988.

Meyer was a speaker on *The Lutheran Hour* radio program from 1989 to 2001. Through 2003, he hosted the national television show *On Main Street* for Lutheran Hour Ministries. In 2001, LHM received two prestigious Emmy awards from the National Academy of Television Arts & Sciences (NATAS) St. Louis/Mid-America Chapter for two *On Main Street* episodes.

Meyer has served The Lutheran Church—Missouri Synod and the church at-large over the years in multiple capacities. He served as third vice-president of the LCMS from 1995 to 1998. He was a charter board member of the Association of Lutheran Older Adults (ALOA), has served as an honorary director of God's Word to the Nations Bible Society and as a member of the Standing Committee on Pastoral Ministry for the LCMS. He was pastoral adviser for the Southern Illinois District of the International Lutheran Laymen's League and has served as first vice president, second vice president, secretary and circuit counselor of the LCMS Southern Illinois District. He served on the Board of Trustees of the American Bible Society from 2001 to 2013.

Meyer has written numerous sermons and columns for Lutheran Hour Ministries, including the booklets "Coping with Cancer" and "Real Men." He co-authored *The Crosses of Lent*, in-depth Bible studies of Matthew and Prophecy in the *LifeLight* series and authored "The Place of the Sermon in the Order of Service" in *Liturgical Preaching* for Concordia Publishing House. He has contributed to *Issues in Christian Education* and is a regular contributor to the *Concordia Journal*. His articles include "A Church Caught in the Middle," "An Urban Seminary," and "Why Go to Church?"

In 2014 Meyer wrote *Timely Reflections: A Minute a Day*

with Dale Meyer, a compilation of 365 daily devotions from his long-running online series, *The Meyer Minute*. This book was published by Tri-Pillar Publishing in conjunction with Concordia Seminary. In 2018, a new volume of his sermons, *Word Alive!*, was published by Tri-Pillar. The volume includes 52 sermons, spanning decades of his ministry.

Meyer has been speaking and preaching for more than 40 years. His areas of interest and study include 1 Peter, the church in a changing culture and the Sabbath applied to life today. He lives in Collinsville, Illinois, with his wife, Diane. They have two grown daughters, Elizabeth (Darren) Pittman and Catharine (Charles) Bailey; and five grandsons, Christian, Connor and Nicholas Pittman, and Andrew and Jacob Bailey.

Rev. Dr. Gerhard C. Michael, Jr.

The son of a pastoral couple, Rev. Dr. Gerhard Michael met his marriage and ministry partner, Joan Westlund, while he was on vicarage. In their more than 50 years of marriage, the Lord has blessed them with six healthy children, two of whom were trained as Lutheran school teachers and have married professional church workers, and one who is serving as a Lutheran pastor, whose wife is also trained as a Lutheran school teacher. The other three children are meaningfully engaged as part of the priesthood of all believers – one as an attorney serving in continuing education, another as a chemical engineer working in research and development, and the third a physical therapist serving as a professor in that area. All are involved in their local congregations. In addition, the Michaels are blessed with 18 grandchildren.

Michael has experienced the call of God's mission in a variety of settings. Seminary field work placed him in an inner-city project; his vicarage experience was in a suburban congregation which had relocated from the inner city. His initial placement after seminary graduation was to serve as a missionary in Japan from 1965–1971, where all Christians combined amounted to 0.5% of the population. When major budget cuts kept Michael from returning to Japan after a year of furlough, he accepted a call to St. John Lutheran Church in Merrill, Wisconsin, where a high percentage of the population was Lutheran. Michael served at St. John from 1971 to 1984.

Following his service in Merrill, Michael accepted a call to a young congregation seeking to establish itself. He served at Mount Calvary Lutheran Church in Warner Robins, Georgia, until 1997. In Georgia, all Lutherans combined amount to 0.5% of the population. In 1997, Michael was elected as President of the Florida-Georgia District and served until 2009. During his tenure, he sought to help each of his congregations see themselves as churches in mission, with each of their members being missionaries.

From 2010 to 2015, Michael headed the Luther Institute – Southeast Asia (LISA), developing a 20-course curriculum, training pastors and teachers, deaconesses and lay leaders in the basics of the Lutheran-Christian faith. Since 2013, he has served as the missionary pastor of St. Peter Lutheran Church in Dahlonega, Georgia, seeking to help it reach out to the people of the North Georgia Mountains. Although the challenges through the years have been varied, what has been the sustaining strength of the ministry has been the grace of our Lord Jesus Christ. Sharing the good news has been a joy and blessing.

During his tenures in Merrill and Warner Robins, Michael served as a volunteer chaplain in the local hospitals. He also served on the initial founding Board of the Merrill Adult Day Care program. In Dahlonega, he has represented the Ministerial Association on the Community Helping Place Board. In Florida he served on the Lutheran Haven Board of Directors in Oviedo, from 2009 to 2015; and on the Board of the Lutheran Services of Florida, from 199 to 2009.

Additionally, he served as the Counselor for the Merrill Circuit from 1976 to 1980; on the Pastoral Conference Planning Committee for three years in the North Wisconsin District and three years in the Florida-Georgia District; as the Pastoral Advisor of the Lutheran Laymen's League, Florida-Georgia District for three years; on the Commission on Theology and Church Relations from 1987 to 1992 and from 2001 to 2009; as a member of the Florida-Georgia District Board of Directors from 1989 to 2009; and as a member of the Garuna Foundation Board of Directors, overseeing missionary work in Southeast Asia, from 2001 to the present.

Michael holds degrees from Concordia College, St. Paul (1959); Concordia Senior College, Fort Wayne (1961); and a Master of Divinity from Concordia Seminary (1965). Additionally, he holds degrees from Harvard Divinity School (1972) with his studies focusing on Japanese religions. He completed additional graduate work at Luther Seminary, St. Paul. In 2003, Concordia College, New York awarded him a Doctor of Humane Letters.

Rev. Dr. Dean Nadasdy

Rev. Dr. Dean Nadasdy is President Emeritus of the Minnesota South District of The Lutheran Church—Missouri Synod, having retired in 2018. His parish experience includes pastorates at Woodbury Lutheran Church, Woodbury, Minnesota (2000–2012); Cross View Lutheran Church, Edina, Minnesota (1981–1997); and Grace Lutheran Church, Eugene, Oregon (1973–1981).

Nadasdy served as a Vice President of the LCMS from 2004 to 2010. He was awarded Doctor of Letters degrees from Concordia University, Nebraska and Concordia University, St. Paul.

From 1997 to 2000 Nadasdy served as Associate Professor of Practical Theology at Concordia Seminary, St. Louis, where he held the Gregg H. Benidt Memorial Chair in Homiletics and Literature. Since 2000 he has continued teaching as an adjunct instructor in the D. Min. program at Concordia Seminary. He is a frequent presenter at pastoral and church worker conferences and has lectured in homiletics at seminaries in Latvia and Hungary. He currently serves as a periodic guest preacher on *The Lutheran Hour.*

Nadasdy has written curriculum (Concordia Publishing House and Augsburg) and is a contributor to *Creative Worship for the Lutheran Parish, Concordia Journal, Concordia Pulpit Resources,* and *Preach the Word.* He also contributed study notes to the *Lutheran Study Bible* (Concordia Publishing House). His published books include *Cross Views: Story Dramas That Teach the Faith* (Concordia Publishing House), *Gospel Dramas* (Augsburg); *Tough Days and Talks with God* (Augsburg); *Questions Teens are Asking Today* (Concordia Publishing

House); and *Preaching is Worship* (Concordia Publishing House). He has chaired Mass Events and Worship Committees for several LCMS National Youth Gatherings. He has written sermon series and devotional booklets for *Creative Communications*, including "The Parables of Lent" (2017) and "The Sermon on the Mount in Lent" (2019). Five of his choral lyrics have been published (Augsburg, MorningStar, and Concordia Publishing House). His most recent book is *The Beautiful Sermon*, on the aesthetics of preaching.

Nadasdy currently chairs the Board of Directors of Feed My Starving Children, a global hunger relief agency based in Minnesota. He is married to Susie, a retired Lutheran middle and high school English and speech teacher. They are blessed with three children, Kristin, Molly, and Philip; and five grandchildren, Luke, Greta, Micah, Emily, and Esther.

Rev. Dr. Robert Newton

Dr. Robert Newton and his wife, Priscilla, grew up together in Napa, California, and have been married 49 years. They have eight children (including in-laws) and 14 grandchildren.

A 1977 graduate of Concordia Theological Seminary, Ft. Wayne, Newton served as an evangelistic missionary to the Kankanaey people in the Philippines from 1977 to 1983. He and his family lived in a remote mountain area of northern Luzon. The ministry involved planting new congregations and preaching stations along with training men to serve as pastors, elders, and evangelists.

The Newtons returned to the United States in July of 1983

so that Newton could pursue graduate studies at the School of World Mission, Fuller Theological Seminary, Pasadena, California. While there, he assisted the Pacific Southwest District in developing a cross-cultural leadership training program. He completed his PhD in 1993 at Trinity Evangelical Divinity School in Deerfield, Illinois.

Newton served as Professor of World Missions at Concordia Theological Seminary from 1985 to 1998. For the 1996–1997 academic year he was on sabbatical with his family serving the Gutnius Lutheran Church in Papua New Guinea under the Board for Mission Services. He assisted as a theological educator at Timothy Lutheran Seminary, while his wife taught classes for the women and hosted retreats and seminars.

In 1998 Newton accepted a call to serve as Senior Pastor to First Immanuel Lutheran Church, an urban, multi-cultural congregation in San Jose, California. He was elected President of the California Nevada Hawaii (CNH) District in 2003 and served in that position until his retirement in 2018.

Rev. Dr. Wilbert J. Sohns

immersion initiator and general author and editor of
The Great Sending: God's Heart Beating Through You

Rev. Dr. Wilbert J. Sohns, a servant of Christ and the Church, was born on October 4, 1933, to Helen Richter and Emil Sohns in Terra Bella, California, He was baptized on October 29, 1933, and confirmed on May 25, 1947, at Zion Lutheran in Terra Bella. After graduation from Zion Lutheran Day School, he attended California Concordia High School and College in Oakland,

California, and went on to attend Concordia Seminary in St. Louis. He was ordained on July 19, 1959, in Cambridge, Nebraska.

He married Lenabell (Lyn) Drosche June 9, 1957, in St. Paul, The Grove, Texas. Their marriage has been blessed with two sons, Stephen (Ursula) and Michael (Julia); six grandchildren, Aaron, David, Ben (Jess), Kristen, Nicole (Jeff), and Connor; and three great-grandchildren, Lincoln, Lenabell, and Adam. Will and his life-long partner served churches in Cambridge, Nebraska; Casper, Wyoming; Broomfield, Colorado; Springfield, Illinois; Cheyenne, Wyoming; and, in retirement, Aleman, Texas.

Sohns served the Lord three terms as President of the Wyoming District, LCMS (1982–1991). During all his years, he served in many other offices, including Circuit Counselor (1962–1968), Pastoral Advisor of the International Lutheran Laymen's League (1968–1972), member and chairman of the LCMS Board for Missions (1973–1982), staff member of the LCMS's Texas District (1992–1995), member and chairman of the LCMS Commission on Constitutional Matters (2002–2013), as well as memberships on many synod committees and task forces. In 1992, he served as the Synodical Convention Chaplain and was a co-founder of *Jesus Is Lord Mission* (Mission Society) in 2002.

During his years of retirement in The Grove, Texas, he has provided numerous articles, essays, and Bible studies to encourage God's mission of being *sent* by Jesus into the world to reach the lost and disciple the saved.

Rev. Dr. Russell L. Sommerfeld

Rev. Russ Sommerfeld was born in Norfolk, Nebraska. His church home was Mount Olive

Lutheran Church. He was educated at Norfolk Senior High School; Concordia College (now University) Saint Paul, Minnesota; Concordia Senior College formerly of Fort Wayne; and Concordia Seminary in Saint Louis. He holds Bachelor, Master of Divinity and Doctor of Letters degrees.

Sommerfeld is married to Donna "Nino" Cargnino of Collinsville, Illinois. "Nino" is a retired registered nurse in psychiatric and dementia care. They have three adult children and four granddaughters.

Sommerfeld served Immanuel and Saint John's Lutheran Churches of Canton and Moundridge, Kansas (1980–1986); Trinity Lutheran Church of Arapahoe, Nebraska (1986–1995); and Holy Cross Lutheran Church and University Lutheran Campus Ministry of Kearney, Nebraska (1995–2003). He also served Nebraska District – LCMS as a Vice President (1994–2003) and as District President (2003–2015). He currently serves as an assistant professor of theology and interim president at Concordia University, Nebraska in Seward, Nebraska.

Sommerfeld was a member of the Regents and the Foundation Board for Concordia University Nebraska, the Lutheran Ministry Foundation and Lutheran Family Services of Nebraska. He loves focusing on Christian outreach in rural and small-town mission and ministry. During his time at the seminary, he was trained in African-American urban ministry. His internship was in chaplaincy at a psychiatric in-patient hospital while also serving a small-town church. Sommerfeld has been given opportunities to have minor roles in the emerging Lutheran churches in Jamaica and the South Sudan of East Africa.

Sommerfeld has enjoyed the diversity of ministerial associations and served as Chairman of the Kearney, Nebraska, Ministerial

Association. He also served as a hospice chaplain, Advisory Board member to the Good Samaritan Health Systems Hospice and Home Health Care of Kearney; and Board member for Buffalo County Community Health Partners. He was a charter member of the Buffalo County Health Ministry Network. Additionally, he served on the national Board of Directors of Wheat Ridge Ministries Now We Raise of Itasca, Illinois. He currently serves on the Board of Directors of Ambassadors of Reconciliation for Billings, Montana. He is a member and past president of the Seward Rotary Club.

He enjoys road bicycling and playing the French Horn, but not at the same time.

Rev. Dr. Larry Stoterau

Rev. Dr. Larry Stoterau was born and raised in Luverne, Minnesota. He graduated from Luverne High School in 1965. He was baptized, confirmed, and later ordained at St. John's Lutheran Church in Luverne. He graduated from Concordia University, St. Paul, in 1967, and from Concordia Senior College, Fort Wayne in 1969, before receiving his Master of Divinity from Concordia Seminary, St. Louis, in 1973. He received a Doctor of Ministry degree from Fuller Theological Seminary, Pasadena, California, in 2001. He met Linda Wuertz in St. Paul and they were married after graduating from college in 1969. In the parish, Stoterau and his wife had the joy of serving together, as she was Director of Worship and Music in both congregations where he served as pastor. Their marriage is blessed with two sons.

From 2000 to 2018 Stoterau served as President of the Pacific Southwest District, leading congregations in southern California, Arizona, and southern Nevada. He pastored Emmaus Lutheran Church, Alhambra, California (1973–1983) and Epiphany Lutheran Church, Chandler, Arizona (1983–2000). He served as Vice Chairman of the Council of Presidents from 2006 to 2009 and Chairman of the Council from 2009 to 2015. He chaired the LCMS Mission 21st-Century Task Force (2002–2005) and was Vice Chairman of the LCMS Task Force on Synod Structure and Governance (2005–2010). He was the Council of President's representative to the Pastoral Leadership Institute (2001–2006) and Concordia University System (2016–2018). He was a member of the Board of Regents, Concordia University, Irvine (2000–2018) and currently serves on the Board of LINC International.

Stoterau is an active community member, having served on the Alhambra Chamber of Commerce Board of Directors and the Alhambra Community Hospital Board of Review. He was active in the Alhambra Kiwanis Club and the Chandler Rotary Club, serving as President.

AN ALTERNATE ORDER OF THE STUDIES

1. Luke 1:46-56; 67-79; 2:8-14; 28-32; 38 – A PROPHESY FULFILLED – THROUGH ORDINARY PEOPLE – Dr. Jerry Kieschnick

2. Mark 1:1-8; Luke 3:3-6; John 1:6-28; 3:1-8; 22-36 – BORN AGAIN... TO BEAR WITNESS TO THE LIGHT – Dr. Jerry Kieschnick

3. Matthew 4:12-22; 9:9-13; Mark 1:14-20; 2:13-17; Luke 5:1-11, 27-32; 6:12-13; John 1:35-51 – CALLING OF THE DISCIPLES/APOSTLES TO CHRIST'S MISSION – Dr. Will Sohns

4. Matthew 10:1-42; Mark 6:7-12; Luke 9:1-9; 10:1-24 – THE DISCIPLES ARE SENT TO THE TOWNS AND VILLAGES – Dr. Dave Buegler

5. Matthew 9:35-38 – FIELDS RIPE FOR HARVEST – Dr. Larry Stoterau

6. Matthew 16:13-20 – WHO DO PEOPLE SAY JESUS IS? – Dr. Larry Stoterau

7. Matthew 18:1-14 – FINDING THE LOST ONE – Dr. Larry Stoterau

8. Matthew 22:1-4; Luke 14:15-24; Revelation 19:6-9 – COME TO THE WEDDING – Dr. Dave Buegler

9. Matthew 20:1-16 – THE LABORERS IN THE VINEYARD – Dr. Dave Buegler

10. Matthew 28:18-20 – RENDEZVOUS WITH JESUS – Dr. Dave Benke

11. Mark 1:1-8 – GOD'S COMMISSION: PROPHESIED – Dr. Paul Maier

12. Luke 4:18-21 – A CHRIST FOR ALL PEOPLE – Dr. Robert Newton

13. Luke 15; Luke 19:1-10 – THE SEEKING GOD – Dr. Robert Newton

14. Luke 24:45-49 – CHRIST COMPLETES IT ALL – Dr. Robert Newton

15. John 1:29-34 – JESUS IS THE SON OF GOD – Rev. Ken Hennings

16. John 3:14-21 – THE MISSION OF GOD IS ACCOMPLISHED THROUGH JESUS – Rev. Ken Hennings

17. John 4:1-42 – GOD'S MISSION AND OURS – Rev. Ken Hennings

18. John 14:16-27; 15:26-27; 16:5-16 – HOLY SPIRIT: DIVNE HELPER– Dr. Dave Benke

19. John chapter 17 – PRAYER DRIVES THE MISSION – Dr. Dean Nadasdy

20. John 18-19 – CHRIST CRUCIFIED – Dr. Dean Nadasdy

21. John 20 – THE SENDING CHRIST – Dr. Dean Nadasdy

22. John 21 – NOURISHING THE FISHERS OF MEN – Dr. Russell Sommerfeld

23. Matthew 28:5-10; Mark 16:6-8; Luke 24:9-12; John 20:2, 17-18 – THE GREAT SENDING – Dr. Paul Maier

24. Acts 1:1-11 – GOD'S MISSION IS OUR MISSION – Dr. Jon Diefenthaler

25. Acts 5:42-6:7 – GOD'S MISSION PARTNERSHIPS – Dr. Jon Diefenthaler

26. Acts 8:1-8 – GOD'S MISSION IS TO THE WHOLE HUMAN FAMILY – Dr. Jon Diefenthaler

27. Acts 10:1-11:18 – GOD'S MISSION WITHOUT WALLS – Rev. Keith Kohlmeier

28. Acts 11:19-30; Acts 13 – OWNING THE NAME – CHRISTIAN – Rev. Keith Kohlmeier

29. Acts 15 – OF COUNCILS, CONFLICT, CONVENTIONS, AND THE MISSION OF GOD – Rev. Keith Kohlmeier

30. Acts 6:7; 9:31; 12:24; 16:5; 19:20; 28:31 – THE MULTIPLICATION

OF THE WORD AND DISCIPLES – Dr. Will Sohns

31. Romans 1:8-16 – THE GOSPEL POWER – Dr. Russell Sommerfeld

32. Romans 10; 16:25-27 – PROCLAIMERS ARE SENT – Dr. Russell Sommerfeld

33. 2 Corinthians 5 – DATE WITH DESTINY – Dr. Dave Benke

34. Philippians 1:12-14, 18b-30; 2:5-11 – THE BASIS FOR OUR BOLDNESS – Dr. Mike Michael

35. 1 Timothy 1:12-2:7 – THE GREAT EXPANSION OF THE FAITH – Dr. Paul Maier

36. Revelation 5:9-10; 1:5-6; Exodus 19:3-8; 1 Peter 2:4-12 – A KINGDOM OF PRIESTS WHO PRAY – Dr. Mike Michael

37. 1 Peter 2:4-12; Ex. 19:3-8; Revelation 1:5-6; 5:9-10 – A KINGDOM OF PRIESTS WHO SERVE – Dr. Mike Michael

38. Isaiah 43:10,12,21; 1 Peter 2:4-10 – A KINGDOM OF PRIESTS WHO WITNESS – Dr. Mike Michael

39. 1 Peter 1:18-25; 2:21-25; 3:18-22 – NOT YET SEEING, BUT BELIEVING AND REJOICING – Dr. Dale Meyer

40. I Peter 1:13-17 – THE FEAR OF GOD – Dr. Dale Meyer

41. 1 Peter 2:4-8 – THE HONOR IS TO YOU WHO BELIEVE – Dr. Dale Meyer

42. Revelation 5:9; 7:9; 10:11; 11:9; 13:7; 14:6; 17:15 – A PANORAMIC VIEW OF GOD'S LOVE FOR THE WORLD – Dr. Will Sohns

ADDITIONAL RATIONALE FOR A JUBILEE IMMERSION

- The *confession of sin*, a genuine life of and an ongoing *repentance*, instead of covering up our missional disobedience resulting in experiencing a "wasting away," "groaning," and being "dried up as the heat of summer" (Psalm 32:1-5).

- A *prayer life* that regularly immerses our being and doing in the Lord when we face the routines of our missional lives, being distracted, being disturbed, and when the church needs a place of solitude, preservation, and deliverance from the consequences of the sins of not embracing Christ AND His mission (Psalm 32:6-7).

- Having had our *transgressions forgiven* and our sins covered by Christ, we submit (immerse in) to the Lord's instruction, teaching, and counsel in contrast to being "like a horse or mule, without understanding, which must be curbed with bit and bridle," and to suffering like "the sorrows of the wicked." With the confessed sin being forgiven and motivated by the steadfast love that surrounds us, the sent confident people of God experience gladness, joy, and an "upright heart" (Psalm 32:8-11).

- "Create in me a clean heart, O God, and renew a right spirit within me. Cast me not away from your presence and take not your Holy Spirit from me. Restore to me the joy of your salvation and uphold me with a willing spirit." —Psalm 51:10-12

- "Whoever believes in me, as the Scripture has said, 'Out of his heart will flow rivers of living water.'" —John 7:38

Life examples

In all of life, but especially made obvious in the world of sports, repetitions (or "reps") are the necessary preparation for a successful athlete. Think of a football quarterback who repeats throws time and again to his receivers for ongoing mental and muscle memory (new habits and renewed eye-to-hand coordination), or a basketball player who practices free throws day in and day out in order to improve. Repetition – repeated action – is required to break old habits of thinking and behavior.

It seems that the church is getting "sacked" again and again with decline, closure of churches, missional apathy, and malaise, locked into tired old programs, habits, mere performances, stopgap measures, and political solutions, with doctrinal conflict, divisiveness, and division.

Athletes must exercise immersion training to break old mental and muscle habits. So it is with Christians who pledge to join God's great sending. Intensive reps in the Word of Christ creates a new spiritual heart and "muscle" memory (a new missional heart transformation at the "free throw line" of the mission to the world).

We can so easily feel trapped behind the locked doors of process, institutional polity, practices, activities, routines, and traditions that we don't realize we must have a long-term immersion to change, transition, and be transformed. Think about how the immediacy of the day and the busyness of the daily grind keep us locked into old habits. It took 40 years for the children of Israel in the wilderness to be transformed under the patience and power of God.

Through the weekly sabbath, the seven-year sabbath (Exodus 16:23; 20:8-11; 35:2; Leviticus 23:3; 25:1-7) and the Jubilee sabbath (Leviticus 25 and 27), God began and regularly continued to refresh, reset, and transform the children of Israel. They were reset in the wilderness to cross the Jordan, and they were transformed again and again in the promised land. Their loving God bore them up on eagles' wings, bringing them to Himself to obey His voice and keep His covenant (see Exodus 19:4-5). Time and again, God called on the Israelites to *be my treasured possession among all peoples, for all the earth is mine; and you shall be to me a kingdom of priests and a holy nation* (Exodus 19:5). In transforming the children of Israel and in repentance, God was resetting their hearts and behavior.

Break the habit of another short-term program, practice, structure change, institutional polity, mere performance, or process-centered activity and instead embrace Christ and His mission requires a complete and holy immersion in His Spirit-filled, heart-transforming, and powerful Word for the sake of His mission. We must cast aside every weight and sin that clings so closely and run with endurance the race set before us (Hebrews 12:1). We must become wholly immersed in His great sending!

OTHER RESOURCES

The following resources are offered as ongoing aids and suggested readings to benefit the continuing exegesis of the Word and world for the sake of Christ's mission.

Commission on Theology and Church Relation essays and related documents

- *"Mission Affirmations,"* LCMS Convention, 1965
- *"The Mission of the Christian Church in the World,"* LCMS, CTCR, 1974
- *"A Theological Statement of Mission,"* LCMS, CTCR, Nov. 1991
- *"Mission Blueprint for the Nineties,"* LCMS, 1992
- *"Missional Churches in a Post-Church World"* (Three Mission Contexts), PPT Presentation by Dr. Robert Newton.

Lutheran Mission Matters

A scholarly journal of *Lutheran Society for Missiology* – a Lutheran forum for the exchange of ideas and discussion of issues related to proclaiming the Gospel of Jesus Christ for an increased participation in God's mission

available at www.lsfm.global

Articles that are particularly helpful include:

- *Those Who Are Sent: Christ and His Church, Christology, Missiology, and Ecclesiology in the Gospel of John,* Robert Kolb, Volume XX, No. 1 (Issue 39), May 2012.

- *As the Father Has Sent Me,* Henry R. Schriever, Volume XX, No. 1 (Issue 39), May 2012.

- *Fresh Wineskins for Christ's Mission,* Robert Newton, Volume XXII, No. 2 (Issue 44), November 2014.

- *Truly Confessional: Responding to the Collapse of Christendom,* Robert Newton, Volume XXIII, No. 1 (Issue 45), May 2015.

- *The Word, the Baptized, and the Mission of God,* Robert Newton, Volume XXIV, No. 1 (Issue 47), January 2016.

- *One Pastor's Efforts to Nurture: A Congregation of Priests,* Gerhard C. Michael, Jr., Volume XXIV, No. 1 (Issue 47), January 2016.

- *Ecclesiology is the Servant of Soteriology,* Robert J. Scudieri, Volume XXIV, No. 2 (Issue 48), May 2016.

- *Recovering the Heart of Mission,* Robert Newton, Volume XXVI, No 1 (52), 2018.

- *The Antioch Model for Faithful Participation in Christ's Mission* Will Sohns, Volume XXVII, No. 1, May 2019.

- *Fear or Faithfulness, Burial or Boldness? Charting the Course for Today's Church on Pause,* Michael Newman, Volume XXVII, No. 1, May 2019.

- *Next Steps for LCMS Multiplication: Two Actions to Reignite a Gospel Movement,* Michael Newman, Volume XXVII, No. 2, November 2019.

Lutheran Hour Ministries

various publications, including those in partnership with The Barna Group and the LHM *SENT* initiative

available at **www.lhm.org**

- *Spiritual Conversations in the Digital Age* (A Barna Group monograph)
- The Reluctant Witness
- How to Talk About Your Faith: An Introduction to the Spiritual Conversation Curve
- The Sent Life: A Study of Sending in the Gospel of John
- Better Together – Monograph
- Many other resources

Articles/Essays/Books

- *The One Holy, Catholic, Apostolic Church,* 1967 LCMS Convention Essay, Dr. Oswald Hoffmann
- *The Mission of God,* Georg Vicedom, CPH, 1965
- *Apostolate and Ministry,* Karl Rengstorf, CPH, 1969
- *Luther on John 17 and John 20,* Luther's Works, Vol. 69
- *Transforming Mission: Paradigm Shifts in Theology of Mission,* David J. Bosch, American Society of Missiology Series, March 20, 1991, November 9, 2011
- *The Mission of God: Unlocking the Bible's Grand Narrative,* Christopher J. H. Wright, InterVarsity Press, Downers Grove, IL: 2006
- *The "Apostolic Church" – One, Holy, Catholic, and Missionary,* Robert J. Scudieri, Mission Nation Publishing, 2016

- *Who Are the Apostles,* Robert J. Scudieri, Mission Nation Publishing, 2015

- *Evangelism in the Early Church,* Michael Green, Eerdmans, revised edition, 2004

- *Father, Son and Spirit: The Trinity and John's Gospel,* Andreas J. Kostenberger and Scott R. Swain, InterVarsity Press, 2008 (especially Chapter Nine, "Toward a Trinitarian Mission Theology", pg. 149)

- *The Missionary Nature of the Church, a Survey of the Biblical Theology of Mission,* Johannes Blauw, McGraw Hill Book Company (printed in Great Britain), 1962

- *The Forgotten Ways [... Apostolic Movements],* Alan Hirsch, Brazos Press (Baker Publishing), 2006, 2016

- *Gospel DNA: Five Markers of a Flourishing Church,* Michael Newman, Ursa Publishing, 2016

- *Canoeing the Mountains,* Tod Bolsinger, IVP Books, 2015; *Study Guide,* IVP Books, 2018

- *"Man Turned in on Himself,"* Heather Choate Davis, a master's thesis from Concordia University, Irvine

- *Best Practices for Church Planting, Best Practices for "Church Planting" Aligned to Missional Disposition/Principles,* 2019, Stephen J. Sohns and Wilbert J. Sohns, see website, www.thegreatsending.org or email: sent@thegreatsending.org

- *"'Knocking on Doors' in Contemporary Society: Practical Implications of 'Sending' for Missional Congregations,"* Wilbert J. Sohns, 2019, see website, www.thegreatsending.org or email: sent@thegreatsending.org

- *Joining Jesus on His Mission,* Greg Finke, , see website, www.dwelling114.org, Tenth Power Publishing, 2014.

- *Loved & Sent,* Jeff Cloeter, Tenth Power Publishing, 2016

Other References and Links:

- **Pastoral Leadership Institute (PLI)** – "PLI trains and invests in multiplying missional leaders and seeks to significantly accelerate a movement of the Gospel by training a global family of 30,000 leaders and churches, for the purpose of multiplying a diverse set of evangelistic communities by 2030."– plileadership.org

- **Mission Partnership Platform** – Concordia Marketplace initiative and the GodWorks initiative – https://missionpartnersplatform.com/

- **Best Practices for Ministry (BPM)** – Christ Church Lutheran, Phoenix, Arizona, Rev. Dr. Jeffrey Schrank, Pastor. BPM goal: "Our goal is that we want to help Christian leaders know that they are not alone." http://www.cclphoenix.org/bpm-resources

- **J2e3** – Concordia Lutheran Church, San Antonio, Texas, Rev. Dr. Bill Tucker, Pastor. J2e3 stands for Jesus to Everyone, Everywhere, Everyday. This initiative began in 2015 and includes connections, resources, and support in the areas of missions, preaching, disaster relief. and more. J2e3.com

- **Mission Nations Publications** – Mission Nation exists to strengthen the church in America by providing resources to help churches reach an ethnic group different from their own. www.MissionNationPublishing.org.

- **Lutheran Bible Translators (LBT)** – Millions of people don't have the Bible in their own language. Many speak a language that is not written down. Lutheran Bible Translators puts God's Word in their hands. www.LBT.org

- **Mission of Christ Network (MCN)** – a lay-led mission organization focused on sending the priesthood of believers to intentionally proclaim the Gospel in cross-cultural settings. MCN trains, sends, and supports missionaries as they serve in God's mission around the world and helps congregations in the US connect to international mission opportunities. MissionofChrist.org

- **Concordia Mission Institute (CMI)** – a joint training platform for equipping the missionaries and staff of Lutheran Bible Translators (LBT) and Mission of Christ Network (MCN) that is grounded in the Biblical truth that all mission belongs to God. CMI is normally a week-long event in July with a growing library of online training. https://www.youtube.com/watch?v=2_N8hYb0tDo

Other Suggested Publications/Subscriptions

Whether you agree or disagree with the content, these reputable and mostly Christian groups and their resources provide information and inspiration via mission thinkers and happenings in Christianity as well as helps in better understanding the world and its cultures:

- 5Q – 5qcentral.com
- ARDA – support@thearda.com
- Barna – barnagroup@barna.com
- Crossway – communications@crossway.org
- Discipleship.org – info@discipleship.org
- Exponential – support@exponential.org
- MissionInsite – missioninsite.com
- Pew Research – info@pewresearch.org

Book Sales

For more purchasing options and information on the book, visit the publisher at www.tenthpowerpublishing.com.

For quantity discounts or general information, contact the author at sent@thegreatsending.org. Visit www.thegreatsending.org.